THE BUDDHA'S TEACHINGS
on SOCIAL *and* COMMUNAL HARMONY

The Buddha's Teachings on Social and Communal Harmony

An Anthology of Discourses
from the Pāli Canon

Edited and introduced by
Bhikkhu Bodhi

Prologue and Epilogue by
Hozan Alan Senauke

Foreword by
H. H. the Dalai Lama

Wisdom

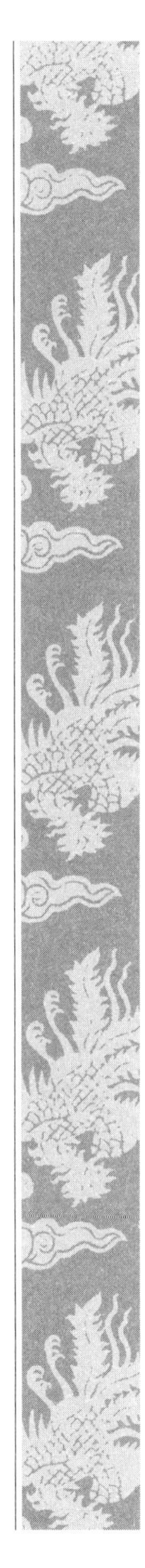

Wisdom Publications
199 Elm Street
Somerville MA 02144 USA
wisdompubs.org
© 2016 Bhikkhu Bodhi

Library of Congress Cataloging-in-Publication Data
Names: Bodhi, Bhikkhu, editor.
Title: The Buddha's teachings on social and communal harmony : an anthology
of discourses from the Pāli Canon / Edited and introduced by Bhikkhu
Bodhi ; Prologue and Epilogue by Hozan Alan Senauke.
Description: Somerville, MA : Wisdom Publications, 2016. | Series: The
teachings of the Buddha | Includes bibliographical references and index.
Identifiers: LCCN 2016008687| ISBN 9781614293552 (paperback) | ISBN
9781614293736 (ebook) | ISBN 1614293554
Subjects: LCSH: Buddhism—Social aspects. | Communalism—Religious
aspects—Buddhism. | BISAC: RELIGION / Buddhism / Sacred Writings. |
RELIGION / Buddhism / Theravada. | RELIGION / Ethics.
Classification: LCC BQ4570.S6 B78 2016 | DDC 294.3/37--dc23
LC record available at https://lccn.loc.gov/2016008687

ISBN 978-1-61429-355-2   ebook ISBN 978-1-61429-373-6

20 19 18 17 16   5 4 3 2 1

Design by Gopa & Ted2, Inc. Set in TeX Gyre Pagella 10/12.4.

Wisdom Publications' books are printed on acid-free paper and meet
the guidelines for permanence and durability of the Production Guidelines
for Book Longevity of the Council on Library Resources.

❀ This book was produced with environmental mindfulness.
For more information, please visit wisdompubs.org/wisdom-environment.

Printed in the United States of America.

Please visit fscus.org.

Contents

Publisher's Acknowledgment

The publisher gratefully acknowledges the generous contribution of the Hershey Family Foundation toward the publication of this book.

Foreword

BY HIS HOLINESS THE DALAI LAMA

The historical Buddha, Shakyamuni, lived, attained enlightenment, and taught in India more than 2,500 years ago. However, I believe that much of what he taught so long ago can be relevant to people's lives today. The Buddha saw that people can live together freely as individuals, equal in principle and therefore responsible for each other.

He saw that the very purpose of life is to be happy. He talked about suffering in the context of ways to overcome it. He recognized that while ignorance binds beings in endless frustration and suffering, the development of understanding is liberating. The Buddha saw that every member of the human family, man and woman alike, has an equal right to liberty, not just in terms of political or even spiritual freedom, but at a fundamental level of freedom from fear and want. He recognized that each of us is just a human being like everyone else. Not only do we all desire happiness and seek to avoid suffering, but each of us has an equal right to pursue these goals.

Within the monastic community that the Buddha established, individuals were equal, whatever their social class or caste origins. The custom of walking on alms round served to strengthen the monks' awareness of their dependence on other people. Within the community, decisions were taken by vote and differences were settled by consensus.

The Buddha took a practical approach to creating a happier, more peaceful world. Certainly he laid out the paths to liberation and enlightenment that Buddhists in many parts of the world continue to follow today, but he also consistently gave advice that anyone may heed to live more happily here and now.

The selections from the Buddha's advice and instructions gathered here in this book—under headings related to being realistic, disciplined, of measured speech, patient rather than angry, considerate of the good of others—all have a bearing on making friends and preserving peace in the community.

We human beings are social animals. Since our future depends on others we need friends in order to fulfil our own interests. We do not make friends by being quarrelsome, jealous, and angry, but by being sincere in our concern for others, protecting their lives, and respecting their rights. Making friends and establishing trust are the basis on which society depends. Like other great teachers the Buddha commended tolerance and forgiveness in restoring trust and resolving disputes that arise because of our tendency to see others in terms of "us" and "them."

In this excellent book Bhikkhu Bodhi, a learned and experienced Buddhist monk, has drawn on the scriptures of the Pāli tradition, one of the earliest records of the Buddha's teachings, to illustrate the Buddha's concern for social and communal harmony. I am sure Buddhists will find the collection valuable, but I hope a wider readership will find it interesting too. The materials gathered here clearly demonstrate that the ultimate purpose of Buddhism is to serve and benefit humanity. Since what interests me is not converting other people to Buddhism, but how we Buddhists can contribute to human society according to our own ideas, I am confident that readers simply interested in creating a happier, more peaceful world will also find it enriching.

The Dalai Lama

Prologue

BY HOZAN ALAN SENAUKE

Gotama Buddha came of age in a land of kingdoms, tribes, and *varna*, meaning social class or caste. It was a time and place both distinct from and similar to our own, in which a person's life was strongly determined by social status, family occupation, cultural identity, and gender. Before the Buddha's awakening, identity was definitive. If one was born into a warrior caste or that of a merchant or a farmer or an outcast, one lived that life completely and almost always married someone from the same class or caste. One's children did the same. There was no sense of individual rights or personal destiny, no way to manifest one's human abilities apart from a societal role assigned at birth. So the Buddha's teaching can be seen as a radical assertion of individual potentiality. Only by one's effort was enlightenment possible, beyond the constraints of caste, position at birth, or conventional reality. In verse 396 of the Dhammapada, the Buddha says:

> I do not call one a brahmin only because of birth, because he is born of a (brahmin) mother. If he has attachments, he is to be called only "self-important." One who is without attachments, without clinging — him do I call a brahmin.

At the same time, the Buddha and his disciples lived in the midst of society. They didn't set up their monasteries on isolated mountaintops but on the outskirts of large cities such as Sāvatthī, Rājagaha, Vesālī, and Kosambī. They depended on laywomen and men, *upāsikā* and *upāsaka*, for the requisites of life. Even today monks and nuns in the Theravāda tradition of Burma (or Myanmar), Thailand, Sri Lanka, Cambodia, and Laos go on morning alms rounds for their food. Although they keep a strict monastic discipline, it is mistaken to imagine that Southeast Asian monasteries are cloistered and apart from their brothers and sisters in the secular world. Monasteries and secular communities are mutually dependent, in a tradition that is sweet and fully alive.

In the autumn of 2007 people around the world were inspired by Burma's determined yet peaceful "Saffron Revolution"—led by a nonviolent protest of Burmese monks against the military government's repression.

The protests were triggered by sudden and radical increases in fuel prices that drastically affected people's ability to get to work or to afford fuel for cooking or even basic foods. The intimate connection between monks, nuns, and laypeople has historically meant that when one sector is suffering, the other responds. Burmese monks have a long history of speaking out against injustice. They have been bold in opposition to British colonialism, dictatorship, and two decades of a military junta.

In Burma Buddhist monks have been agents of change in a society that stands on the brink of real transformation. While this change is inevitable, the military junta had previously resisted it with grim determination. A confluence of circumstances created an opening: the election of a new civilian government (however one might question the electoral process), the release of political prisoners (including Nobel laureate Daw Aung San Suu Kyi after many years of house arrest), nonviolent movements around the world encouraged by 2011's "Arab Spring," and a new dialogue between Burma's leaders and representatives from Europe, the United States, and other economic powers. There was a feeling of possibility and hope in the air.

This anthology underscores living within the Dhamma in a free and harmonious society, using the Buddha's time-tested words. Returning from Burma in November of 2011, I had been thinking about the need there and elsewhere for this kind of collection from the Pāli suttas. In 2012 communal violence erupted in Burma's Rakhine State and elsewhere in that country. A need to look deeply into the Buddha's teachings on social harmony has become urgent. Not being a scholar or a translator, I contacted several learned friends. It turns out that several years back Bhikkhu Bodhi, one of our most respected and prolific interpreters of Early Buddhism, had assembled such a collection as an addendum to a training curriculum for social harmony in Sri Lanka, organized by the Institute for the Study of Human Rights at Columbia University.

Here is the Buddha's advice about how to live harmoniously in societies that are not oppressing those of different religions or ethnic backgrounds, not savaging and exploiting themselves or others. While circumstances in Burma, Sri Lanka, Thailand, India, or the United States vary, the Buddha's social teachings offer a kind of wisdom that transcends the particularities of time and place. His teachings provide a ground of liberation upon which each nation and people can build according to its own needs.

I am most grateful to Bhikkhu Bodhi for his wisdom and generosity. People of all faiths and beliefs in every land yearn for happiness and liberation. I honor those who move toward freedom, and hope that the Buddha's words on social harmony may lead us fearlessly along our path.

Berkeley, CA

List of Abbreviations

AN	Aṅguttara Nikāya
CDB	Connected Discourses of the Buddha
Dhp	Dhammapada
DN	Dīgha Nikāya
It	Itivuttaka
LDB	Long Discourses of the Buddha
MLDB	Middle Length Discourses of the Buddha
MN	Majjhima Nikāya
NDB	Numerical Discourses of the Buddha
SN	Saṃyutta Nikāya
Sn	Suttanipāta
Ud	Udāna
Vin	Vinaya Piṭaka
Vism	Visuddhimagga

Available translations

Aṅguttara Nikāya: *The Numerical Discourses of the Buddha*, translated by Bhikkhu Bodhi. Boston: Wisdom Publications, 2012.

Dhammapada: *The Dhammapada, The Buddha's Path of Wisdom*, translated by Acharya Buddharakkhita. 2nd edition. Kandy, Sri Lanka: Buddhist Publication Society, 1996.

Dīgha Nikāya: *The Long Discourses of the Buddha*, translated by Maurice Walshe. Boston: Wisdom Publications, 1995.

Majjhima Nikāya: *The Middle Length Discourses of the Buddha*, translated by Bhikkhu Ñāṇamoli, edited by Bhikkhu Bodhi. 3rd ed. Boston: Wisdom Publications, 2005. (Originally published 1995.)

Saṃyutta Nikāya: *The Connected Discourses of the Buddha*, translated by Bhikkhu Bodhi. Boston: Wisdom Publications, 2000.

Suttanipāta: *The Suttanipāta*, translated by Bhikkhu Bodhi (in preparation).

Udāna and Itivuttaka: *The Udāna and the Itivuttaka: Inspired Utterances of the Buddha and The Buddha's Sayings*, translated by John D. Ireland. Kandy, Sri Lanka: Buddhist Publication Society, 1997.

Vinaya Piṭaka: *The Book of Discipline*, translated by I. B. Horner. 6 volumes. London: Pali Text Society (1969–75).
Visuddhimagga: *The Path of Purification*, translated by Bhikkhu Ñāṇamoli. Colombo, Sri Lanka: M. D. Gunasena, 1964.

All translations in this anthology are taken from the volumes listed above. Several passages have been slightly revised.

Key to the Pronunciation of Pāli

The Pāli Alphabet
Vowels: a, ā, i, ī, u, ū, e, o

Consonants
Gutterals   k, kh, g, gh, ṅ
Palatals   c, ch, j, jh, ñ
Cerebrals   ṭ, ṭh, ḍ, ḍh, ṇ
Dentals   t, th, d, dh, n
Labials   p, ph, b, bh, m
Other   y, r, ḷ, l, v, s, h, ṃ

Pronunciation
a as in "cut"
ā as in "father"
i as in "king"
ī as in "keen"
u as in "put"
ū as in "rule"
e as in "way"
o as in "home"

Of the vowels, *e* and *o* are long before a single consonant and short before a double consonant. Among the consonants, *g* is always pronounced as in "good," *c* as in "church," *ñ* as in "onion." The cerebrals (or retroflexes) are spoken with the tongue on the roof of the mouth; the dentals with the tongue on the upper teeth. The aspirates—*kh, gh, ch, jh, ṭh, ḍh, th, dh, ph, bh*—are single consonants pronounced with slightly more force than the nonaspirates, e.g., *th* as in "Thomas" (not as in "thin"); *ph* as in "putter" (not as in "phone"). Double consonants are always enunciated separately, e.g., *dd* as in "mad dog," *gg* as in "big gun." The pure nasal (*niggahīta*) *ṃ* is pronounced like the *ng* in "song." An *o* and an *e* always carry a stress; otherwise the stress falls on a long vowel—*ā, ī, ū,* or on a double consonant, or on *ṃ*.

Acknowledgments

In 2011 Bhikkhu Khemaratana shared with me an outline of texts from the Pāli Canon that he had prepared on the theme of monastic harmony, a topic in which he has been particularly interested. The texts that I have chosen for several sections of this anthology were suggested by those selected by Ven. Khemaratana, though my treatment of the topic has been governed by the purpose of this anthology and thus differs from his outline. I am also grateful to Alan Senauke for writing a prologue and epilogue to this volume, drawing upon his own experience using the earlier version of this anthology in his work of fostering social harmony and reconciliation in India and Myanmar.

Detailed List of Contents

General Introduction

THE ORIGINS OF THE BUDDHA'S TEACHINGS ON SOCIAL HARMONY

Conflict and violence have plagued humankind from time immemorial, leaving the annals of history stained with blood. While the human heart has always stirred with the yearning for peace, harmony, and loving fellowship, the means of satisfying this yearning have ever proved elusive. In international relations, wars succeed one another like scenes in a film, with only brief pauses during which the hostile powers set about forging new alliances and making surreptitious grabs for territory. Social systems are constantly torn by class struggles, in which the elite class seeks to amass more privileges and the subordinate class to achieve greater rights and more security. Whether it is the conflict between masters and slaves, between feudal lords and serfs, between the aristocrats and the common people, between capital and labor, it seems that only the faces change while the underlying dynamics of the power struggle remain the same. Communities as well are constantly threatened by internal strife. Rival bids for power, differences of opinion, and competing interests among their members can tear them apart, giving birth to new cycles of enmity. When each new war, division, or dispute has peaked, the hope rises that reconciliation will follow, that peace and unity will eventually prevail. Yet, again and again, these hopes are quickly disappointed.

A moving passage in the scriptures of Early Buddhism testifies to this disparity between our aspirations for peace and the stark reality of perpetual conflict. On one occasion, it is said, Sakka, the ruler of the gods, visited the Buddha and asked the anguished question: "Why is it that when people wish to live in peace, without hatred or enmity, they are everywhere embroiled in hatred and enmity?" (see **Text VIII,1**). The same question rings down the ages, and it could be asked with equal urgency about many troublespots in today's world: Iraq and Syria, the Gaza Strip, the Central African Republic and South Sudan, Myanmar and Sri Lanka, Charleston and Baltimore.

This problem must also have weighed on the Buddha's heart as he traveled the Ganges plain on his teaching tours. The society of his time was divided into separate castes distinguished by the prerogatives of the elite and the servile status of those at the bottom. Those outside the caste system, the outcasts, were treated even worse, subjected to the most degrading indignities. The political landscape, too, was changing, as monarchies led by ambitious kings rose from the ashes of the older tribal states and embarked on military campaigns intended to expand their domains. Within the courts personal rivalries among those hungry for power were bitter. Even the spiritual communities of the time were not immune to conflict. Philosophers and ascetics proud of their theories sparred with each other in passionate debates, each seeking to defeat their rivals and swell the ranks of their followers.

In a deeply moving poem in the Suttanipāta (vv. 935–37) the Buddha gives voice to the feeling of vertigo such violence had produced in him, perhaps soon after he left Kapilavatthu and witnessed firsthand the world outside his native land:

> Fear has arisen from one who has taken up violence:
> behold the people engaged in strife.
> I will tell you of my sense of urgency,
> how I was stirred by a sense of urgency.
>
> Having seen people trembling
> like fish in a brook with little water,
> when I saw them hostile to one another,
> fear came upon me.
>
> The world was insubstantial all around;
> all the directions were in turmoil.
> Desiring an abode for myself,
> I did not see any place unoccupied.

Once he began teaching, the Buddha's primary mission was to make known the path that culminates in inner peace, in the supreme security of nibbāna, release from the cycle of birth, old age, and death. But the Buddha did not turn his back on the human condition in favor of a purely ascetic, introspective quest for liberation. From his position as a renunciant who stood outside the conventional social order, he looked with deep concern on struggling humanity, enmeshed in conflict while aspiring for peace, and out of compassion he sought to bring harmony into the troubled arena of human relations, to promote a way of life based on tolerance, concord, and kindness.

But he did even more. He founded an intentional community devoted to fostering inner and outer peace. This task was thrust upon him almost from the start; for the Buddha was not a solitary wanderer, teaching those who came to him for guidance and then leaving them to their own devices. He was the founder of a new spiritual movement that from the outset was inevitably communal. Immediately after he concluded his first sermon, the five ascetics who heard it asked to become his disciples. As time went on, his teaching attracted increasing numbers of men and women who chose to follow him into the life of homelessness and take on the full burden of his training. Thus a *Sangha*—a community of monks and nuns who lived in groups, traveled in groups, and trained in groups—gradually developed around him.

Changing from their lay garments into ocher robes, however, was not an immediate passport to holiness. While their way of life had altered, the monks and nuns who entered the Buddha's order still brought along with them the ingrained human tendencies toward anger, pride, ambition, envy, self-righteousness, and opinionatedness. It was thus inevitable that tensions within the monastic community would arise, develop at times into outright antagonism, and spawn factionalism, strife, and even bitter conflict. For the Sangha to flourish, the Buddha had indeed to become an "organization man." While he could proclaim high spiritual ideals toward which his disciples could strive, this was not sufficient to ensure harmony in the Sangha. He also had to establish a detailed code of regulations for the uniform performance of communal functions and to promulgate rules that would restrain if not totally obliterate divisive tendencies. These became the *Vinaya*, the body of monastic discipline.

The Buddha also taught and guided people who chose to follow his teachings at home, as lay disciples, living in the midst of their families and working at their regular occupations. He was thus faced with the additional task of laying down guidelines for society as a whole. In addition to a basic code of lay precepts, he had to offer principles to ensure that parents and children, husbands and wives, employers and employees, and people from very different backgrounds and social classes would be able to live together amicably. In the face of these challenges the scope of the Dhamma expanded. From its original character as a path to spiritual liberation, centered around contemplative practices and philosophical insights, it gave rise to a broad ethic that applied not only to individual conduct but to the relations between people living under diverse conditions, whether in monasteries or at home, whether pursuing their livelihoods in the marketplace or workshop or in the service of the state. Under all these circumstances, the chief ethical requirement was the avoidance of harm: harm through aggression, harm by trampling on the claims of others, harm through conflict and violence. The ideal was to promote good will and harmony in action, speech, and thought.

The Structure of This Book

The present anthology is intended to bring to light the Buddha's teachings on social and communal harmony. It is based on a selection of texts I compiled in 2011 at the request of the Program on Peace-building and Rights of the Institute for the Study of Human Rights at Columbia University, intended for use among Buddhist monks in Sri Lanka in the aftermath of the country's long ethnic conflict that ended in 2009. This expanded version includes new texts and changes in the arrangement.

The texts are all taken from the Pāli Canon, the body of scriptures regarded as authoritative "Word of the Buddha" (*buddha-vacana*) by followers of Theravāda Buddhism, the school of Buddhism that prevails in the countries of southern Asia—primarily Sri Lanka, Burma, Thailand, Cambodia, and Laos. The passages I have drawn upon come exclusively from the Sutta Piṭaka, the Discourse Collection, which contains the discourses of the Buddha and his eminent disciples. I did not include texts from the other two collections, the Vinaya Piṭaka, the Collection on Monastic Discipline, and the Abhidhamma Piṭaka, the Collection of Doctrinal Treatises. While parts of the Vinaya Piṭaka may have been relevant to this project, the bulk of material in that corpus is concerned with monastic rules and regulations and thus would be more relevant to a specialized readership. Further, those passages of the Vinaya broadly concerned with communal harmony have parallels in the Sutta Piṭaka that have been included here.

Although the Pāli Canon is the authorized scriptural collection of Theravāda Buddhism, the texts of this anthology need not be regarded as narrowly tied to any particular school of Buddhism, for they come from the oldest stratum of Buddhist literature, from collections of discourses that stand at the fountainhead of Buddhism. Nor are these teachings necessarily bound up with any creed or system of religious belief. In their clarity, cogency, and deep understanding of human nature, they should be able to speak to anyone regardless of religious affiliation. The texts have a universal message that makes them applicable to all endeavors to promote amiable relations between people. They provide perceptive diagnoses of the underlying roots of conflict, simply and clearly expressed, and offer practical strategies for resolving disputes, promoting reconciliation, and establishing social harmony.

I have arranged the selections according to a structure that deliberately mirrors, in certain respects, patterns that the Buddha himself adopted in expounding his teaching. In the rest of this general introduction I will explain the logic underlying my arrangement. Each part begins with its own introduction, which is intended to tie together the texts in that chapter and make explicit their connection to the chapter's theme.

Part I consists of texts on right view or right understanding. The Buddha made right view the first factor of the noble eightfold path and elsewhere stressed the role of right view as a guide to the moral and spiritual life. Since the objective of the present anthology is to provide a Buddhist perspective on communal harmony rather than to show the path to final liberation, the texts I have included here highlight the type of right understanding that fosters ethical conduct. This is sometimes called "mundane right view"—in contrast to "world-transcending right view," the penetrative insight into the empty and essenceless nature of all conditioned things that severs the roots of bondage to the cycle of rebirths.

Right understanding of the principle of kamma has a decisive impact on one's conduct. When we realize that our own deeds eventually rebound on ourselves and determine our destiny in future lives, we will be motivated to abandon defiled mental qualities and abstain from bad conduct. Instead, we will be inspired to engage in good conduct and develop wholesome qualities. This pattern is reflected in the structure of the noble eightfold path itself, where right view leads to right intentions, which are in turn manifested in right speech, right action, and right livelihood.

In Part II, I treat the impact of right understanding on the individual under the heading of "personal training." Early Buddhism sees personal transformation as the key to the transformation of society. A peaceful and harmonious society cannot be imposed from the outside by the decrees of a powerful authority but can only emerge when people rectify their minds and adopt worthy standards of conduct. Thus the task of promoting communal harmony must begin with personal transformation. Personal transformation occurs through a process of training that involves both outward displays of good conduct and inner purification. Following the traditional Buddhist scheme, I subsume this course of personal transformation under the three headings of generosity, ethical self-discipline, and cultivation of the mind.

The chief obstacle to social harmony is anger or resentment. Anger is the seed from which enmity grows, and thus, in the process of personal training, the Buddha gave special attention to controlling and removing anger. I have therefore devoted Part III to "Dealing with Anger." The texts included reveal the grounds from which anger arises, the drawbacks and dangers in yielding to anger, and the practical antidotes that can be used to remove anger. The main remedy for anger is patience, which the Buddha enjoins even under the most trying circumstances. Thus the last two sections in the chapter comprise texts dealing with patience, both as injunctions and through stories about those who best exemplify patience.

Part IV is devoted to speech. Speech is an aspect of human conduct whose role in relation to social harmony is so vital that the Buddha made right speech a distinct factor in the noble eightfold path. I have followed the Buddha's example by devoting an extensive selection of texts to the subject of speech. These deal not only with right speech as usually understood but also with the proper way to participate in debates, when to praise and criticize others, and how to correct a wrongdoer when the need arises.

With Part V, we move more explicitly from the sphere of personal cultivation to interpersonal relations. These relations begin with good friendship, a quality the Buddha stressed as the basis for the good life. In the texts I selected, we see the Buddha explain to both his monastic disciples and lay followers the value of associating with good friends, delineate the qualities of a true friend, and describe how friends should treat one another. He relates good friendship to both success in the household life and the spiritual development of the monk.

Part VI expands the scope of the inquiry from personal friendship to wider spheres of influence. In this chapter I include a selection of texts in which the Buddha highlights the social implications of personal conduct. The chapter begins with passages that contrast the foolish person and the wise person, the bad person and the good person. The chapter then goes on to compare those practitioners who are devoted solely to their own good with those who are also devoted to the good of others. The texts consider this dichotomy from the perspectives of both monastic and lay practitioners. What emerges is a clear confirmation that the best course of practice is one dedicated to the twofold good: one's own and that of others.

Part VII brings us to the establishment of an intentional community. Since the Buddha was the founder of a monastic order, not a secular ruler, the guidelines he proposes for establishing community naturally pertain primarily to monastic life. But on occasion he was requested by civil leaders to provide advice on maintaining harmony in society at large, and the principles he laid down have been preserved in the discourses. Other selections in this chapter are concerned with cooperation between the two branches of the Buddhist community, the monastics and the laity.

Nevertheless, even when they act with the best intentions, people bring along with them tendencies that lead to factionalism and disputes. Disputes form the subject of Part VIII. The texts included here deal with internal disputes among both monastics and laity, which in some respects have similar origins but in other respects spring from different causes. This part leads naturally into Part IX, which is devoted to the means of resolving disputes. Here we see the Buddha in his role as a monastic legislator, laying down guidelines for settling conflicts and proposing modes of training to prevent disputes from erupting in the future.

Part X, the last in this anthology, moves from the intentional community, as represented by the monastic order, to the larger social domain. Its theme is the establishment of an equitable society. I here include passages from the discourses that explore the interwoven and overlapping relationships that constitute the fabric of society. The texts include the Buddha's teachings on family life, on the relations between parents and children and husbands and wives, and the maintenance of a beneficent home life. The last part of this chapter deals with the Buddha's political ideals, which are represented by the figure of the "wheel-turning monarch," the *rājā cakkavattī*, the righteous ruler who administers his realm in harmony with the moral law. Although principles of governance laid down for a monarch might seem obsolete in our present age with its professed commitment to democracy, in their emphasis on justice, benevolence, and righteousness as the basis for political authority, these ancient Buddhist texts still have contemporary relevance.

I. Right Understanding

Introduction

The Buddha taught that right understanding, or "right view," is the forerunner on the path to liberation. He assigned right view to the position of first factor of the noble eightfold path, the way to the end of suffering, and held that all the other factors of the path must be guided by right view toward the goal of his teaching, the cessation of suffering. For the Buddha, however, right view plays a critical role not only on the path to liberation but also in the attainment of well-being and happiness within the cycle of rebirths. It does this by underscoring the need for ethical conduct. The type of right view integral to the moral life is sometimes called "mundane right view" (*lokiya-sammādiṭṭhi*) or "the right view of one's personal responsibility for one's deeds" (*kammassakatā sammādiṭṭhi*). This kind of right view is based on the premise that there is an objective, transcendent basis for morality that is not dependent on human judgments and opinions. Through his enlightenment, the Buddha discovered this moral law and derived from it the specific ethical injunctions of his teaching.

On the basis of this discovery, the Buddha holds that the validity of moral distinctions is built into the fabric of the cosmos. Moral judgments can be distinguished as true and false, actions determined as good and bad, with reference to a moral law that is just as efficacious, just as universal in its operation, as the laws of physics and chemistry. As moral agents, therefore, we cannot justify our actions simply by appeal to personal preferences, nor can we expect following our preferences to secure our well-being. Rather, to achieve true well-being, we must act in conformity with the moral law, which is the Dhamma itself, the fundamental principle of truth and goodness that abides whether or not buddhas discover it and reveal it.

Right view affirms that our morally significant actions have consequences that can bring us either happiness or misery. Our deeds create *kamma*, a force with the potential to produce results that correspond to the ethical quality of the original action. Kamma brings forth "fruits," retributive consequences that reflect the actions from which they spring. The basic principle that underlies the working of kamma is that good deeds bring desirable fruits, conducing to good fortune and happiness, while evil deeds bring undesirable fruits, leading to misfortune and suffering. Thus the results of our volitional deeds are not limited to their immediately visible effects, those that spring from purely naturalistic chains of causation. There is an invisible principle of moral causation operating behind the scenes such that, with the passage of time, whether long or short, our actions eventually return to us and determine our destiny in this life and in future lives.

The Buddha contrasts right view of the efficacy of kamma with three types of wrong view that were promulgated by iconoclastic thinkers of his age.[1] One type of wrong view, called the doctrine of moral nihilism (*natthikavāda*), denies personal survival beyond death and says that there are no fruits of our good and bad deeds. At death, both the foolish and the wise are utterly annihilated, leaving behind only a physical corpse. A second kind of wrong view, called the doctrine of non-doing (*akiriyavāda*), denies that there is a valid basis for making moral distinctions. Those who engage in such horrific deeds as slaughtering and tormenting others cannot be said to be doing wrong; those who give generously and protect the helpless cannot be said to be acting rightly. The distinction between evil deeds and meritorious deeds is a human fabrication, purely subjective, and thus moral judgments are mere projections of personal opinions. The third type of wrong view, called the doctrine of non-causality (*ahetukavāda*), proclaims that there is no cause or reason for the defilement of beings and no cause or reason for the purification of beings. Beings are defiled and purified without any cause. They do not have moral agency, the capacity to determine their own destiny, but are compelled to act as they do by fate, circumstance, and nature.

The Buddha expounded his conception of right view as the response to these three types of wrong view. He taught that personal identity survives bodily death, and the form we assume in each existence is determined by our kamma. Living beings pass through a beginningless series of rebirths in the course of which they reap the fruits of their good and bad deeds. The fact that our own deeds return to us thus provides a strong incentive to abstain from evil and pursue the good. In contrast to the doctrine of non-doing, the Buddha held that moral judgments are not arbitrary. They have an objective basis, so that certain actions—such as killing and stealing—can be rightly described as evil, while other types of conduct—such as giving and moral restraint—can be rightly described as good. And the Buddha held that there are indeed causes for the defilement and purification of beings. People are not driven helplessly by fate but have the capacity for self-determination. Through heedlessness we defile ourselves and by diligent effort we can purify ourselves. The determinants of our destiny lie within ourselves and are subject to our own volitional control.

Harmony in any community, whether a small group or a whole society, depends on a shared commitment to ethical conduct. While there can be harmony among thieves, such harmony can only last as long as the thieves are honest with each other, and for this reason, the unity of such groups generally turns out to be short-lived. As philosophers have long recognized, true community depends on a shared commitment to virtue. Since the Buddha held that ethical conduct rests on a foundation of right view, it follows that a modicum of right understanding is critical to fostering a harmonious community. In the present age, however, when the critical method of science has given rise to skepticism about conscious survival of death, it would be presumptuous to insist that a full acceptance of right view as taught by the Buddha is necessary as a foundation for social harmony. It seems, though, that social harmony requires at minimum that the members of any group share the conviction that there are objective standards for distinguishing between good and bad conduct and that there are benefits, for the group and its individual members, in avoiding the types of behavior generally considered bad and in living according to standards generally considered good. Several texts testify that the Buddha himself seems to have recognized that morality can be established on the basis of self-reflection and ethical reasoning without requiring a belief in personal survival of death.

In Part I, I have assembled a number of suttas that describe the nature of right view. The texts I have chosen emphasize the view of one's personal responsibility for one's actions rather than the right view that leads to liberation. **Text I,1** draws a pair of distinctions that run through the Buddha's teachings. The passage begins by highlighting the role of right view as the forerunner of the path, whose first task is to distinguish between wrong view and right view. Thus right view not only understands the actual nature of things, but it also distinguishes between wrong and right opinions about the nature of things. In this passage, the Buddha describes wrong view with the stock formula for the view of moral nihilism. In defining right view, he draws a second distinction, that between right view that is still "subject to the influxes," which is the view of one's ownership of one's actions, and the "world-transcending" right view that pertains to the noble eightfold path. Right view subject to the influxes, also called mundane right view, distinguishes between the unwholesome and the wholesome. It lays bare the underlying roots of good and bad conduct and affirms the principles behind the operation of kamma, the law of moral causation which ensures that good and bad deeds eventually produce their appropriate fruits. Although this kind of right view, on its own, does not lead to liberation, it is essential for progress within the cycle of rebirths and serves as the foundation for the world-transcending right view, which eradicates ignorance and the associated defilements.

Mundane right view is the understanding of the efficacy of kamma.

Through mundane right view, one understands that unwholesome kamma, deeds arisen from impure motives, eventually redound upon oneself and bring suffering, a bad rebirth, and spiritual deterioration. Conversely, one understands that wholesome kamma, deeds arisen from virtuous motives, leads to happiness, a fortunate rebirth, and spiritual progress. In **Text I,2**, the Venerable Sāriputta enumerates the courses of unwholesome kamma and their underlying roots, as well as the courses of wholesome kamma and their roots. Unwholesome kamma is explicated by way of the "ten courses of unwholesome action." The roots of unwholesome kamma, the motives from which it originates, are greed, hatred, and delusion. In contrast, wholesome kamma is explicated by way of the ten courses of wholesome action, which include the right view of kamma and its fruits. The wholesome roots are said to be non-greed, non-hatred, and non-delusion, which may be expressed more positively as generosity, loving-kindness, and wisdom.

Text I,3 offers a more detailed analysis of kamma. In this passage, the Buddha declares that the essential factor in the creation of kamma is volition or intention (*cetanā*), for it is the intention that imparts to the action its moral quality. He also explains the diversity of kamma by way of its capacity to lead to rebirth in different realms of existence; these are the five destinations according to the cosmology of Early Buddhism. According to the suttas, kamma brings its fruits not only in the human realm but in any among the five destinations. Unwholesome kamma leads to rebirth in the three lower realms—the hells, the animal realm, and the realm of afflicted spirits; wholesome kamma brings rebirth in the two higher realms—the human world and the deva world or heavens. Kamma is further differentiated according to the period in which it comes to fruition: some actions bear their fruit in this life itself; others are bound to bring results in the next life; and still others are capable of ripening in any life subsequent to the next one.

Further clarification on the operation of kamma is provided by **Text I,4**, in which the Buddha explains to a brahmin the three clear knowledges he attained on the night of his enlightenment. The second was the knowledge of the divine eye, with which he could directly see how beings pass from death to new birth in accordance with their kamma. Those who engage in misconduct pass on to states of misery; those who engage in good conduct pass on to happy states. The general principle that emerges from this account is the close correlation between our deeds and their results. Across the gap of lifetimes, kamma bears fruits that mirror the original deeds from which they spring. Thus those who take life create kamma that leads to a short lifespan, those who protect life create kamma that leads to a long lifespan; a similar principle holds sway over other types of action.

While the Buddha promoted ethics on the basis of the view of the moral efficacy of action—the principle that good actions lead to desirable results and bad actions to undesirable results—he also offered independent grounds for the ethical life. Thus, while recognizing the law of kamma serves as an incentive for moral behavior, acceptance of karmic causation is not necessary as a justification for ethics. The need for ethical behavior can be established on other grounds that do not presuppose a belief in postmortem survival. These grounds can be reached through personal reflection.

In the Kālāma Sutta, cited in part here as **Text I,5**, the Buddha asks the Kālāmas of Kesaputta, who were uncertain whether there is an afterlife, to suspend judgments about such matters and to recognize directly for themselves, by self-reflection, that acting on the basis of greed, hatred, and delusion leads to harm and suffering for oneself and others; while, in contrast, freeing the mind of greed, hatred, and delusion and acting in beneficent ways brings well-being and happiness to both oneself and others. In another sutta, again partly cited here at **Text I,6**, the Buddha grounds the basic types of right action, such as abstaining from killing and stealing, on a course of moral reflection by which one places oneself in the position of others and decides how to act after considering how one would feel if others were to treat oneself in such ways. Although the Buddha is here responding to a question about the means to a heavenly rebirth, he does not expressly ground moral injunctions on the law of kamma or survival of death but on the principle of reciprocity. This principle, explained in detail here, is succinctly expressed by a verse in the Dhammapada: "All beings tremble at violence, all fear death. Putting oneself in the place of another, one should not kill or cause another to kill" (v. 129).

I. Right Understanding

1. Right View Comes First

"Monks, right view comes first. And how does right view come first? One understands wrong view as wrong view and right view as right view: this is one's right view.

"And what is wrong view? 'There is nothing given, nothing sacrificed, nothing offered; there is no fruit or result of good and bad actions; there is no this world, no other world; there is no mother, no father; there are no beings spontaneously reborn; there are in the world no ascetics and brahmins of right conduct and right practice who, having realized this world and the other world for themselves by direct knowledge, make them known to others.' This is wrong view.

"And what is right view? Right view, I say, is twofold: there is right view that is affected by influxes, partaking of merit, ripening in the acquisitions; and there is right view that is noble, free of influxes, supramundane, a factor of the path.[2]

"And what is right view that is subject to the influxes, partaking of merit, ripening in the acquisitions? 'There is what is given, sacrificed, and offered; there is fruit and result of good and bad actions; there is this world and the other world; there is mother and father; there are beings spontaneously reborn; there are in the world ascetics and brahmins of right conduct and right practice who, having realized this world and the other world for themselves by direct knowledge, make them known to others.' This is right view that is subject to the influxes, partaking of merit, ripening in the acquisitions.

"And what is right view that is noble, free of influxes, supramundane, a factor of the path? The wisdom, the faculty of wisdom, the power of wisdom, the investigation-of-states enlightenment factor, the path factor of right view in one whose mind is noble, whose mind is without influxes, who possesses the noble path and is developing the noble path: this is right view that is noble, free of influxes, supramundane, a factor of the path.

"One makes an effort to abandon wrong view and to enter upon right view: this is one's right effort. Mindfully one abandons wrong view, mindfully one enters upon and abides in right view: this is one's right mindfulness. Thus these three states run and circle around right view, that is, right view, right effort, and right mindfulness."

(from MN 117, MLDB 934–35)

2. Understanding the Unwholesome and the Wholesome

[The Venerable Sāriputta said:] "When, friends, a noble disciple understands the unwholesome and the root of the unwholesome, the wholesome and the root of the wholesome, in that way he is one of right view, whose view is straight, who has perfect confidence in the Dhamma and has arrived at this true Dhamma.

"And what, friends, is the unwholesome, what is the root of the unwholesome, what is the wholesome, what is the root of the wholesome? The destruction of life is unwholesome; taking what is not given is unwholesome; sexual misconduct is unwholesome; false speech is unwholesome; divisive speech is unwholesome; harsh speech is unwholesome; idle chatter is unwholesome; covetousness is unwholesome; ill will is unwholesome; wrong view is unwholesome. This is called the unwholesome. And what is the root of the unwholesome? Greed is a root of the unwholesome; hatred is a root of the unwholesome; delusion is a root of the unwholesome. This is called the root of the unwholesome.

"And what is the wholesome? Abstention from the destruction of life is wholesome; abstention from taking what is not given is wholesome; abstention from sexual misconduct is wholesome; abstention from false speech is wholesome; abstention from divisive speech is wholesome; abstention from harsh speech is wholesome; abstention from idle chatter is wholesome; non-covetousness is wholesome; benevolence is wholesome; right view is wholesome. This is called the wholesome. And what is the root of the wholesome? Non-greed is a root of the wholesome; non-hatred is a root of the wholesome; non-delusion is a root of the wholesome. This is called the root of the wholesome."

(from MN 9, MLDB 132–33)

3. A Miscellany on Kamma

[The Buddha is addressing the monks:] "When it was said: 'Kamma should be understood, the source and origin of kamma should be understood, the diversity of kamma should be understood, the result of kamma should be understood, the cessation of kamma should be understood, and the way leading to the cessation of kamma should be understood,' for what reason was this said?

"It is volition, monks, that I call kamma. For having willed, one acts by body, speech, or mind.

"And what is the source and origin of kamma? Contact is its source and origin.

"And what is the diversity of kamma? There is kamma to be experienced in hell; kamma to be experienced in the animal realm; kamma to be experienced in the realm of afflicted spirits; kamma to be experienced in the human world; and kamma to be experienced in the deva world. This is called the diversity of kamma.

"And what is the result of kamma? The result of kamma, I say, is threefold: [to be experienced] in this very life, or in the [next] rebirth, or on some subsequent occasion. This is called the result of kamma.

"And what, monks, is the cessation of kamma? With the cessation of contact there is cessation of kamma.

"This noble eightfold path is the way leading to the cessation of kamma, namely, right view . . . right concentration.

"When, monks, a noble disciple thus understands kamma, the source and origin of kamma, the diversity of kamma, the result of kamma, the cessation of kamma, and the way leading to the cessation of kamma, he understands this penetrative spiritual life to be the cessation of kamma."

(from AN 6:63, NDB 963)

4. Beings Fare According to Their Kamma

[The Buddha is speaking to a brahmin:] "When, brahmin, my mind was thus concentrated, purified, cleansed, unblemished, rid of defilement, malleable, wieldy, steady, and attained to imperturbability, I directed it to the knowledge of the passing away and rebirth of beings. With the divine eye, which is purified and surpasses the human, I saw beings passing away and being reborn, inferior and superior, beautiful and ugly, fortunate and unfortunate, and I understood how beings fare in accordance with their kamma thus: 'These beings who engaged in misconduct by body, speech, and mind, who reviled the noble ones, held wrong view, and undertook action based on wrong view, with the breakup of the body, after death, have been reborn in the plane of misery, in a bad destination, in the lower world, in hell; but these beings who engaged in good conduct by body, speech, and mind, who did not revile the noble ones, who held right view, and undertook action based on right view, with the breakup of the body, after death, have been reborn in a good destination, in the heavenly world.' Thus with the divine eye, which is purified and surpasses the human, I saw beings passing away and being reborn, inferior and superior, beautiful and ugly, fortunate and unfortunate, and I understood how beings fare in accordance with their kamma. This was the second clear knowledge attained by me in the middle watch of the night. Ignorance was dispelled, clear knowledge had arisen; darkness was dispelled, light had arisen, as happens when one dwells heedful, ardent, and resolute. This, brahmin, was my second breaking out, like that of the chick breaking out of the eggshell."

(AN 8:11, NDB 1128–29)

5. When You Know for Yourselves

The Kālāmas of Kesaputta approached the Blessed One and said to him: "Bhante, there are some ascetics and brahmins who come to Kesaputta. They explain and elucidate their own doctrines, but disparage, denigrate, deride, and denounce the doctrines of others. But then some other ascetics and brahmins come to Kesaputta, and they too explain and elucidate their own doctrines, but disparage, denigrate, deride, and denounce the doctrines of others. We are perplexed and in doubt, Bhante, as to which of these good ascetics speak truth and which speak falsehood."

"It is fitting for you to be perplexed, Kālāmas, it is fitting for you to be in doubt. Doubt has arisen in you about a perplexing matter. Come, Kālāmas, do not go by oral tradition, by lineage of teaching, by hearsay, by a collection of scriptures, by logical reasoning, by inferential reasoning, by reasoned cogitation, by the acceptance of a view after pondering it, by the seeming competence [of a speaker], or because you think: 'The ascetic is our guru.' But when, Kālāmas, you know for yourselves: 'These things are unwholesome; these things are blameworthy; these things are censured by the wise; these things, if accepted and undertaken, lead to harm and suffering,' then you should abandon them.

"What do you think, Kālāmas? When greed, hatred, and delusion arise in a person, is it for his welfare or for his harm?" – "For his harm, Bhante." – "Kālāmas, one overcome by greed, hatred, and delusion, with mind obsessed by them, destroys life, takes what is not given, transgresses with another's wife, and speaks falsehood; and he encourages others to do likewise. Will that lead to his harm and suffering for a long time?" – "Yes, Bhante."

"What do you think? Are these things wholesome or unwholesome?" – "Unwholesome, Bhante." – "Blameworthy or blameless?" – "Blameworthy, Bhante." – "Censured or praised by the wise?" – "Censured by the wise, Bhante." – "Accepted and undertaken, do they lead to harm and suffering or not, or how do you take it?" – "Accepted and undertaken, these things lead to harm and suffering. So we take it."

"Thus, Kālāmas, when we said: 'Come, Kālāmas, do not go by oral tradition. . . . But when you know for yourselves: "These things are unwholesome; these things are blameworthy; these things are censured by the wise;

these things, if undertaken and practiced, lead to harm and suffering," then you should abandon them,' it is because of this that this was said.

"Come, Kālāmas, do not go by oral tradition . . . or because you think: 'The ascetic is our guru.' But when you know for yourselves: 'These things are wholesome; these things are blameless; these things are praised by the wise; these things, if accepted and undertaken, lead to welfare and happiness,' then you should live in accordance with them.

"What do you think, Kālāmas? When a person is without greed, hatred, and delusion, is it for his welfare or for his harm?" – "For his welfare, Bhante." – "Kālāmas, a person not overcome by greed, hatred, and delusion, whose mind is not obsessed by them, does not destroy life, take what is not given, transgress with another's wife, or speak falsehood; nor does he encourage others to do likewise. Will that lead to his welfare and happiness for a long time?" – "Yes, Bhante."

"What do you think, Kālāmas? Are these things wholesome or unwholesome?" – "Wholesome, Bhante." – "Blameworthy or blameless?" – "Blameless, Bhante." – "Censured or praised by the wise?" – "Praised by the wise, Bhante." – "Accepted and undertaken, do they lead to welfare and happiness or not, or how do you take it?" – "Accepted and undertaken, these things lead to welfare and happiness. So we take it."

"Thus, Kālāmas, when we said: 'Come, Kālāmas, do not go by oral tradition. . . . But when you know for yourselves: "These things are wholesome; these things are blameless; these things are praised by the wise; these things, if accepted and undertaken, lead to welfare and happiness," then you should live in accordance with them,' it is because of this that this was said."

(from AN 3:65, NDB 280–82)

6. A Teaching Applicable to Oneself

The householders of Bamboo Gate said to the Blessed One: "Please teach us the Dhamma in such a way that we might dwell happily at home and after death be reborn in a good destination, in a heavenly world."

"I will teach you, householders, a Dhamma exposition applicable to oneself. Listen to that and attend closely, I will speak." – "Yes, sir," those brahmin householders of Bamboo Gate replied. The Blessed One said this:

"What, householders, is the Dhamma exposition applicable to oneself? Here, householders, a noble disciple reflects thus: 'I am one who wishes to live, who does not wish to die; I desire happiness and am averse to suffering. Since I am one who wishes to live . . . and am averse to suffering, if someone were to take my life, that would not be pleasing and agreeable to me. Now if I were to take the life of another—of one who wishes to live, who does not wish to die, who desires happiness and is averse to suffering—that would not be pleasing and agreeable to the other. What is displeasing and disagreeable to me is displeasing and disagreeable to the other too. How can I inflict upon another what is displeasing and disagreeable to me?' Having reflected thus, he himself abstains from the destruction of life, exhorts others to abstain from the destruction of life, and speaks in praise of abstinence from the destruction of life. Thus this bodily conduct of his is purified in three respects.

"Again, householders, a noble disciple reflects thus: 'If someone were to take from me what I have not given, that is, to commit theft, that would not be pleasing and agreeable to me. Now if I were to take from another what he has not given, that is, to commit theft, that would not be pleasing and agreeable to the other. What is displeasing and disagreeable to me is displeasing and disagreeable to the other too. How can I inflict upon another what is displeasing and disagreeable to me?' Having reflected thus, he himself abstains from taking what is not given, exhorts others to abstain from taking what is not given, and speaks in praise of abstinence from taking what is not given. Thus this bodily conduct of his is purified in three respects.

"Again, householders, a noble disciple reflects thus: 'If someone were to commit adultery with my wife, that would not be pleasing and agreeable to me. Now if I were to commit adultery with the wife of another, that would not be pleasing and agreeable to the other. What is displeasing and disagreeable to me is displeasing and disagreeable to the other too. How can I inflict upon another what is displeasing and disagreeable to me?' Having reflected thus, he himself abstains from sexual misconduct, exhorts others to abstain from sexual misconduct, and speaks in praise of abstinence from sexual misconduct. Thus this bodily conduct of his is purified in three respects.

"Again, householders, a noble disciple reflects thus: 'If someone were to damage my welfare with false speech, that would not be pleasing and agreeable to me. Now if I were to damage the welfare of another with false speech, that would not be pleasing and agreeable to the other. What is displeasing and disagreeable to me is displeasing and disagreeable to the other too. How can I inflict upon another what is displeasing and disagreeable to me?' Having reflected thus, he himself abstains from false speech, exhorts others to abstain from false speech, and speaks in praise of abstinence from false speech. Thus this verbal conduct of his is purified in three respects.

"Again, householders, a noble disciple reflects thus: 'If someone were to divide me from my friends by divisive speech, that would not be pleasing and agreeable to me. Now if I were to divide another from his friends by divisive speech, that would not be pleasing and agreeable to the other. . . .' Thus this verbal conduct of his is purified in three respects.

"Again, householders, a noble disciple reflects thus: 'If someone were to address me with harsh speech, that would not be pleasing and agreeable to me. Now if I were to address another with harsh speech, that would not be pleasing and agreeable to the other. . . . ' Thus this verbal conduct of his is purified in three respects.

"Again, householders, a noble disciple reflects thus: 'If someone were to address me with frivolous speech and idle chatter, that would not be pleasing and agreeable to me. Now if I were to address another with frivolous speech and idle chatter, that would not be pleasing and agreeable to the other. What is displeasing and disagreeable to me is displeasing and disagreeable to the other too. How can I inflict upon another what is displeasing and disagreeable to me?' Having reflected thus, he himself abstains from idle chatter, exhorts others to abstain from idle chatter, and speaks in praise of abstinence from idle chatter. Thus this verbal conduct of his is purified in three respects."

(from SN 55:7, CDB 1797–99)

II. Personal Training

Introduction

The Buddha teaches that our views influence all other aspects of our lives. The influence begins with the impact of our views upon our motivation. In the structure of the eightfold path, wrong view is the condition for wrong motivation, for intentions governed by lust, ill will, and violence, while right view is the condition for right motivation, for intentions governed by non-attachment, benevolence, and compassion.[1] The Buddha compares wrong view to a bitter seed, from which there inevitably arise bitter plants (AN 10:104, NDB 1485): "Just as a seed of neem, bitter cucumber, or bitter gourd, planted in moist soil and receiving water, would all lead to fruits with a bitter flavor, so for a person of wrong view . . . whatever bodily action, verbal action, and mental action he undertakes in accordance with that view, and whatever his volition, yearning, inclination, and activities, all lead to harm and suffering. For what reason? Because the view is bad." Right view, in contrast, is like the seed of a sweet plant: "Just as a seed of sugar cane, hill rice, or grape, planted in moist soil and receiving water, would all lead to fruits with a sweet and delectable flavor, just so, for a person of right view . . . whatever bodily action, verbal action, and mental action he undertakes in accordance with that view, and whatever his volition, yearning, inclination, and volitional activities, all lead to well-being and happiness. For what reason? Because the view is good."

Thus when we adopt wrong view, that view shapes our intentions in ways that manifest as unwholesome attitudes and bad actions. For the Buddha, the motivation to behave morally is undercut by the belief that there is no personal existence beyond death, no valid distinctions between good and bad deeds, and no freedom to choose between the right and the wrong. In contrast, the motivation to behave morally is buttressed by the belief that death does not mark the complete end of personal existence, that there are valid distinctions between good and bad deeds, and that our destiny is not rigidly determined by external forces. But the process of personal transformation does not occur automatically. For right view to exercise a positive influence, personal effort is required, a deliberate endeavor to harmonize our conduct with our understanding and intentions.

The texts included in Part II illustrate the transformative impact of right view and right intentions on conduct. I have organized the passages in accordance with a traditional classification of meritorious action into three classes: giving, virtuous behavior, and mental cultivation (*dāna, sīla, bhāvanā*). This corresponds with the Buddha's own method of expounding the Dhamma, in which he begins with generosity, proceeds to good conduct, and then, when the listener is ready, teaches the four noble truths and the eightfold path.

I begin with suttas that highlight different aspects of generosity or giving. Generosity (*cāga*) might be seen as an expression of the right intention of renunciation. It is the antidote to miserliness, an outgrowth of attachment, which, as **Text II,1(1)** shows, is a reluctance to share one's possessions, friends, and even knowledge with others. As the opposite of miserliness, generosity, as stated in **II,1(2)**, issues forth in the act of giving (*dāna*), by which one relinquishes attachment to things and delights in sharing them with others. Giving thereby creates bonds of solidarity with others and fosters a sense of mutual support.

Giving can be practiced for different reasons, but as **Text II,1(3)** states, the foremost reason for giving is "for the purpose of ornamenting the mind." The act of giving can also be performed in different ways, but according to **Text II,1(4)**, it is best when based on faith, done respectfully, at the right time, with a generous heart, and importantly, without denigrating the recipient. Giving particularly means offering to those in need the things that might alleviate their plight. **Texts II,1(5)** and **II,1(6)** say that chief among material gifts is the gift of food, but superior to all material gifts, states **II,1(7)**, is the gift of the Dhamma.

The key to virtuous behavior (*sīla*), according to **Text II,2(1)**, is moral introspection; that is, inward self-inspection of the likely consequences of one's intended actions. Here, the Buddha teaches his son, the novice Rāhula, that before acting one should reflect on the impact one's action is likely to have upon oneself and others. One's decision to reject the action or to pursue it should accord with the result of one's reflections, on whether it is likely to lead to harm for oneself and others or to bring benefits for oneself and others. This already introduces a social dimension into one's private moral deliberations. The other-regarding component, however, is to be balanced by an "enlightened self-interest" that rests on considering the effect of one's intended action on oneself. One is not to do good for others in ways that compromise one's own moral integrity.

Virtuous behavior itself is cultivated by undertaking precepts and acting in accordance with the ten courses of wholesome action. The five precepts (*pañcasīla*) constitute the most fundamental moral code taught by the Buddha: abstaining from killing, stealing, sexual misconduct, false speech, and the use of intoxicants. Following these precepts, according to **Text II,2(2)**, is called accomplishment in virtuous behavior. A broader moral code, which includes as well inward attitudes and right view, is laid out in the ten courses of wholesome action, which expand the requirements of right speech and also include mental orientations. The precepts and courses of wholesome action regulate bodily and verbal conduct, ensuring that we do not inflict harm on others. They also mold our intentions so that we recognize what kind of attitudes lead to conflict and disharmony and replace them with benign intentions that promote concord. **Text II,2(3)** shows that the benefits of observing the precepts do not accrue solely to oneself but extend to countless others, giving "an immeasurable number of beings freedom from fear, enmity, and affliction." Thus virtuous behavior unifies self-benefit and the benefiting of others; it merges the imperative of enlightened self-interest with that of ethical altruism.

Running parallel with the adoption of wholesome conduct is the endeavor of inner cultivation. Mental cultivation involves a double process aimed at shifting the mind away from defiled emotions and at generating mental qualities conducive to lightness, purity, and inner peace. Since many of the Buddha's discourses deal with these two processes, I have had to limit my selection to texts that seem most relevant to promoting social harmony.

Text II,3(1), an excerpt from the Simile of the Cloth, enjoins the removal of sixteen mental defilements. On inspection it will be seen that virtually all these defilements—states such as greed and ill will, anger and hostility, envy and miserliness—have wide-ranging social ramifications. Thus the process of mental training, while bringing inner purification, simultaneously conduces to social harmony.

In an autobiographical discourse partly cited as **Text II,3(2)**, the Buddha explains how, when he was striving for enlightenment, he divided his thoughts into two categories—the good and the bad—and then used appropriate reflection to eliminate the bad thoughts and cultivate the good thoughts. His reflections take into account not only the effect his thoughts would have on himself but also their impact on others. The bad thoughts are those that lead to harm for others, the good thoughts are those that are harmless. **Text II,3(3)** explains the process of what is called "effacement" (*sallekha*), the removal of unwholesome qualities, as the relinquishment of forty-four defilements, a comprehensive scheme that includes several subsidiary groups such as the five hindrances, the ten wrong courses of action, and others.

Along with the elimination of defilements, the training of the mind involves the cultivation of virtuous qualities. Among the virtues most crucial to establishing social harmony are those comprised under the "four immeasurables" (*appamaññā*) or the "four divine abodes" (*brahmavihāra*): loving-kindness, compassion, altruistic joy, and equanimity.[2] **Text II,4(1)** is the standard canonical formula for the four immeasurables. As defined by the Pāli commentaries, loving-kindness is the wish for the welfare and happiness of all beings; compassion is the desire to remove suffering; altruistic joy is gladness at the success and good fortune of others; and equanimity is impartiality and freedom from bias.[3]

As the foundation for the other three, loving-kindness receives the most attention in the Nikāyas. I reflect this emphasis by highlighting loving-kindness in **Texts II,4(2)–(5)**. We here see the Buddha praise the development of loving-kindness as the foremost of meritorious deeds pertaining to the cycle of rebirths. It creates affection in others and ensures self-protection. It leads to higher rebirth and serves as a condition for the extinction of defilements. Among all virtuous qualities, wisdom is considered supreme, for wisdom alone can permanently uproot the ignorance and craving that tie us to the cycle of birth and death. Nevertheless, as **Text II,4(5)** indicates, loving-kindness and the four foundations of mindfulness, the practice that leads to wisdom, are not mutually exclusive but can be developed in unison. It is by cultivating the foundations of mindfulness and generating wisdom that one protects oneself; it is by loving-kindness that one protects others. Finally, **Text II,4(6)** shows how meditative absorption on loving-kindness can be used as a basis for developing insight and reaching the final goal, the unshakable liberation of mind that comes with the destruction of defilements.

II. Personal Training

1. GENEROSITY

(1) Miserliness

"There are, monks, these five kinds of miserliness. What five? Miserliness with regard to dwellings, miserliness with regard to families, miserliness with regard to gains, miserliness with regard to praise, and miserliness with regard to the Dhamma. These are the five kinds of miserliness. Of these five kinds of miserliness, the vilest is miserliness with regard to the Dhamma. The spiritual life is lived for the abandoning and eradication of these five kinds of miserliness."

(AN 5:254–55, NDB 839)

(2) Accomplishment in Generosity

"What is accomplishment in generosity? Here, a noble disciple dwells at home with a mind free from the stain of miserliness, freely generous, open-handed, delighting in relinquishment, devoted to charity, delighting in giving and sharing. This is called accomplishment in generosity."

(from AN 4:61, NDB 450)

(3) Reasons for Giving

"There are, monks, eight reasons for giving. What eight? (1) One gives a gift from desire. (2) One gives a gift from hatred. (3) One gives a gift from delusion. (4) One gives a gift from fear. (5) One gives a gift, thinking: 'Giving was practiced before by my father and forefathers; I should not abandon this ancient family custom.' (6) One gives a gift, thinking: 'Having given this gift, with the breakup of the body, after death, I will be reborn in a good destination, in a heavenly world.' (7) One gives a gift, thinking: 'When I am giving this gift my mind becomes placid, and elation and joy arise.' (8) One gives a gift for the purpose

31

of ornamenting the mind, equipping the mind. These are the eight grounds for giving."

(AN 8:33, NDB 1166)

(4) A Superior Person's Gifts

"There are, monks, these five gifts of a superior person. What five? He gives a gift out of faith; he gives a gift respectfully; he gives a gift at the right time; he gives a gift with a generous heart; he gives a gift without denigration.

(1) "Because he gives a gift out of faith, wherever the result of that gift ripens he becomes rich, affluent, and wealthy, and he is handsome, comely, graceful, endowed with supreme beauty of complexion.

(2) "Because he gives a gift respectfully, wherever the result of that gift ripens he becomes rich, affluent, and wealthy, and his children and wives, his servants, messengers, and workers are obedient, lend their ears to him, and apply their minds to understand him.

(3) "Because he gives a gift at the right time, wherever the result of that gift ripens he becomes rich, affluent, and wealthy, and benefits come to him at the right time, in abundant measure.

(4) "Because he gives a gift with a generous heart, wherever the result of that gift ripens he becomes rich, affluent, and wealthy, and his mind inclines to the enjoyment of excellent things among the five cords of sensual pleasure.

(5) "Because he gives a gift without denigrating himself and others, wherever the result of that gift ripens he becomes rich, affluent, and wealthy, and no loss of his wealth takes place from any quarter, whether from fire, floods, the king, bandits, or unloved heirs.

"These, monks, are the five gifts of a superior person."

(AN 5:148, NDB 763–64)

(5) The Gift of Food (1)

"Monks, if people knew, as I know, the result of giving and sharing, they would not eat without having given, nor would they allow the stain of miserliness to obsess them and take root in their minds. Even if it were their last morsel, their last mouthful, they would not eat without having shared it, if there were someone to share it with. But, monks, as people do not know, as I know, the result of giving and sharing, they eat without having given, and the stain of miserliness obsesses them and takes root in their minds."

(It §26)

(6) The Gift of Food (2)

"A woman noble disciple, by giving food, gives four things to the recipients. What four? She gives long life, beauty, happiness, and strength. By giving long life, she herself will be endowed with long life, human or divine. By giving beauty, she herself will be endowed with beauty, human or divine. By giving happiness, she herself will be endowed with happiness, human or divine. By giving strength, she herself will be endowed with strength, human or divine. A woman noble disciple, by giving food, gives those four things to the recipients."

(AN 4:57, NDB 447)

(7) The Gift of the Dhamma

"Monks, there are these two kinds of gifts. What two? The gift of material goods and the gift of the Dhamma. Of these two kinds of gifts, the gift of the Dhamma is foremost. There are these two kinds of offerings . . . these two kinds of generosity . . . these two objects of relinquishment. What two? The relinquishment of material goods and relinquishment [by giving] the Dhamma. These are the two kinds of relinquishment. Of these two kinds of relinquishment, relinquishment [by giving] the Dhamma is foremost."

(AN 2:141–44, NDB 182)

2. Virtuous Behavior

(1) Moral Introspection

"What do you think, Rāhula? What is the purpose of a mirror?"

"For the purpose of reflection, Bhante."

"So too, Rāhula, an action with the body should be done after repeated reflection; an action by speech should be done after repeated reflection; an action by mind should be done after repeated reflection.

"Rāhula, when *you wish to do an action with the body*, you should reflect upon that same bodily action thus: 'Would this action that I wish to do with the body lead to my own affliction, or to the affliction of others, or to the affliction of both? Is it an unwholesome bodily action with painful consequences, with painful results?' When you reflect, if you know: 'This action that I wish to do with the body would lead to my own affliction, or to the affliction of others, or to the affliction of both; it is an unwholesome bodily action with painful consequences, with painful results,' then you definitely should not do such an action with the body. But when you reflect, if you know: 'This action that I wish to do with the body would not lead to my own affliction, or to the affliction of others, or to the affliction of both; it is a wholesome bodily action with pleasant consequences, with pleasant results,' then you may do such an action with the body.

"Also, Rāhula, *while you are doing an action with the body*, you should reflect upon that same bodily action thus: 'Does this action that I am doing with the body lead to my own affliction, or to the affliction of others, or to the affliction of both? Is it an unwholesome bodily action with painful consequences, with painful results?' When you reflect, if you know: 'This action that I am doing with the body leads to my own affliction, or to the affliction of others, or to the affliction of both; it is an unwholesome bodily action with painful consequences, with painful results,' then you should suspend such a bodily action. But when you reflect, if you know: 'This action that I am doing with the body does not lead to my own affliction, or to the affliction of others, or to the affliction of both; it is a wholesome bodily action with pleasant consequences, with pleasant results,' then you may continue in such a bodily action.

"Also, Rāhula, *after you have done an action with the body*, you should reflect upon that same bodily action thus: 'Did this action that I did with the body lead to my own affliction, or to the affliction of others, or to the affliction of both? Was it an unwholesome bodily action with painful consequences, with painful results?' When you reflect, if you know: 'This action that I did with the body led to my own affliction, or to the affliction of others, or to the affliction of both; it was an unwholesome bodily action with painful consequences, with painful results,' then you should confess such a bodily action, reveal it, and lay it open to the Teacher or to your wise companions in the holy life. Having confessed it, revealed it, and laid it open, you should undertake restraint for the future. But when you reflect, if you know: 'This action that I did with the body did not lead to my own affliction, or to the affliction of others, or to the affliction of both; it was a wholesome bodily action with pleasant consequences, pleasant results,' you can abide happy and glad, training day and night in wholesome states."[4]

(MN 61, MLDB 524–26)

(2) Accomplishment in Virtuous Behavior

"What, monks, is accomplishment in virtuous behavior? Here, a noble disciple abstains from the destruction of life, abstains from taking what is not given, abstains from sexual misconduct, abstains from false speech, abstains from liquor, wine, and intoxicants, the basis for heedlessness. This is called accomplishment in virtuous behavior."

(from AN 4:61, NDB 449–50)

(3) Protecting Countless Beings

"Here, a noble disciple, having abandoned the destruction of life, abstains from the destruction of life. By abstaining from the destruction of life, the noble disciple gives to an immeasurable number of beings freedom from fear, enmity, and affliction. He himself in turn enjoys immeasurable freedom from fear, enmity, and affliction. This is the first gift, a great gift, primal, of long standing, traditional, ancient, unadulterated and never before adulterated, which is not being adulterated and will not be adulterated, not repudiated by wise ascetics and brahmins.

"Again, a noble disciple, having abandoned the taking of what is not given, abstains from taking what is not given. By abstaining from taking what is not given, the noble disciple gives to an immeasurable number of beings freedom from fear, enmity, and affliction. He himself in turn enjoys immeasurable freedom from fear, enmity, and affliction. This is the second gift. . . .

"Again, a noble disciple, having abandoned sexual misconduct, abstains from sexual misconduct. By abstaining from sexual misconduct, the noble disciple gives to an immeasurable number of beings freedom from fear, enmity, and affliction. He himself in turn enjoys immeasurable freedom from fear, enmity, and affliction. This is the third gift. . . .

"Again, a noble disciple, having abandoned false speech, abstains from false speech. By abstaining from false speech, the noble disciple gives to an immeasurable number of beings freedom from fear, enmity, and affliction. He himself in turn enjoys immeasurable freedom from fear, enmity, and affliction. This is the fourth gift. . . .

"Again, a noble disciple, having abandoned liquor, wine, and intoxicants, abstains from liquor, wine, and intoxicants, the basis for heedlessness. By abstaining from liquor, wine, and intoxicants, the noble disciple gives to an immeasurable number of beings freedom from fear, enmity, and affliction. He himself in turn enjoys immeasurable freedom from fear, enmity, and affliction. This is the fifth gift, a great gift, primal, of long standing, traditional, ancient, unadulterated and never before adulterated, which is not being adulterated and will not be adulterated, not repudiated by wise ascetics and brahmins."

(from AN 8:39, NDB 1174)

(4) The Bad and the Good

"Monks, I will teach you what is good and what is bad. And what is the bad? The destruction of life, taking what is not given, sexual misconduct, false speech, divisive speech, harsh speech, idle chatter, covetousness, ill will, and wrong view. This is called the bad.

"And what is the good? Abstention from the destruction of life, abstention from taking what is not given, abstention from sexual misconduct, abstention from false speech, abstention from divisive speech, abstention from harsh speech, abstention from idle chatter, non-covetousness, benevolence, and right view. This is called the good."

(AN 10:178, NDB 1526)

(5) Impurity and Purity

"Impurity by body, Cunda, is threefold. Impurity by speech is fourfold. Impurity by mind is threefold.

"And how is impurity by body threefold? (1) Here, someone destroys life. He is murderous, bloody-handed, given to blows and violence, merciless to living beings. (2) He takes what is not given. He steals the wealth and property of others in the village or forest. (3) He engages in sexual misconduct. He has sexual relations with women who are protected by their mother, father, mother and father, brother, sister, or relatives; who are protected by their Dhamma; who have a husband; whose violation entails a penalty; or even with one already engaged. It is in this way that impurity by body is threefold.

"And how, Cunda, is impurity by speech fourfold? (1) Here, someone speaks falsehood. If he is summoned to a council, to an assembly, to his relatives' presence, to his guild, or to the court, and questioned as a witness thus: 'So, good man, tell what you know,' then, not knowing, he says, 'I know,' or knowing, he says, 'I do not know'; not seeing, he says, 'I see,' or seeing, he says, 'I do not see.' Thus he consciously speaks falsehood for his own ends, or for another's ends, or for some trifling worldly end. (2) He speaks divisively. Having heard something here, he repeats it elsewhere in order to divide those people from these; or having heard something elsewhere, he repeats it to these people in order to divide them from those. Thus he is one who divides those who are united, a creator of divisions, one who enjoys factions, rejoices in factions, delights in factions, a speaker of words that create factions. (3) He speaks harshly. He utters such words as are rough, hard, hurtful to others, offensive to others, bordering on anger, unconducive to concentration. (4) He indulges in idle chatter. He speaks at an improper time, speaks falsely, speaks what is unbeneficial, speaks contrary to the Dhamma and the discipline; at an improper time he speaks such words as are worthless, unreasonable, rambling, and unbeneficial. It is in this way that impurity by speech is fourfold.

"And how, Cunda, is impurity by mind threefold? (1) Here, someone is full of covetousness. He longs for the wealth and property of others thus: 'Oh, may what belongs to another be mine!' (2) He has a mind of ill will and intentions of hate thus: 'May these beings be slain, slaughtered, cut off, destroyed, or annihilated!' (3) He holds wrong view and has an incorrect perspective thus: 'There is nothing given, nothing sacrificed, nothing offered; there is no fruit or result of good and bad actions; there is no this world, no other world; there is no mother, no father; there are no beings spontaneously reborn; there are in the world no ascetics and brahmins of right conduct and right practice who, having realized this world and the other world for themselves by direct knowledge, make them known to others.' It is in this way that impurity by mind is threefold."

"These, Cunda, are the ten courses of unwholesome kamma. . . . It is because people engage in these ten courses of unwholesome kamma that hell, the animal realm, the sphere of afflicted spirits, and any other bad destinations are seen.

"Purity by body, Cunda, is threefold. Purity by speech is fourfold. Purity by mind is threefold.

"And how, Cunda, is purity by body threefold? (1) Here, someone, having abandoned the destruction of life, abstains from the destruction of life. With the rod and weapon laid aside, conscientious and kindly, he dwells compassionate toward all living beings. (2) Having abandoned the taking of what is not given, he abstains from taking what is not given. He does not steal the wealth and property of others in the village or in the forest. (3) Having abandoned sexual misconduct, he abstains from sexual misconduct. He does not have sexual relations with women who are protected by their mother, father, mother and father, brother, sister, or relatives; who are protected by their Dhamma; who have a husband; whose violation entails a penalty; or even with one already engaged. It is in this way that purity by body is threefold.

"And how, Cunda, is purity by speech fourfold? (1) Here, someone, having abandoned false speech, abstains from false speech. If he is summoned to a council, to an assembly, to his relatives' presence, to his guild, or to the court, and questioned as a witness thus: 'So, good man, tell what you know,' then, not knowing, he says, 'I do not know,' or knowing, he says, 'I know'; not seeing, he says, 'I do not see,' or seeing, he says, 'I see.' Thus he does not consciously speak falsehood for his own ends, or for another's ends, or for some trifling worldly end. (2) Having abandoned divisive speech, he abstains from divisive speech. Having heard something here, he does not repeat it elsewhere in order to divide those people from these; or having heard something elsewhere, he does not repeat it to these people in order to divide them from those. Thus he is one who reunites those who are divided, a promoter of unity, who enjoys concord, rejoices in concord, delights in concord, a speaker of words that promote concord. (3) Having abandoned harsh speech, he abstains from harsh speech. He speaks such words as are gentle, pleasing to the ear, and lovable, as go to the heart, are courteous, desired by many, and agreeable to many. (4) Having abandoned idle chatter, he abstains from idle chatter. He speaks at a proper time, speaks truth, speaks what is beneficial, speaks on the Dhamma and the discipline; at a proper time he speaks such words as are worth recording, reasonable, succinct, and beneficial. It is in this way that purity by speech is fourfold.

"And how, Cunda, is purity by mind threefold? (1) Here, someone is without covetousness. He does not long for the wealth and property of others thus: 'Oh, may what belongs to another be mine!' (2) He is benevolent and his intentions are free of hate thus: 'May these beings live happily, free from enmity, affliction, and anxiety!' (3) He holds right view and has a correct perspective thus: 'There is what is given, sacrificed, and offered; there is fruit and result of good and bad actions; there is this world and the other world; there is mother and father; there are beings spontaneously reborn; there are in the world ascetics and brahmins of right conduct and right practice who, having realized this world and the other world for themselves by direct knowledge, make them known to others.' It is in this way that purity by mind is threefold."

"These, Cunda, are the ten courses of wholesome kamma. . . . It is because people engage in these ten courses of wholesome kamma that the devas, human beings, and any other good destinations are discerned."

(from AN 10:176, NDB 1519–22)

3. REMOVING THE DEFILEMENTS OF THE MIND

(1) Sixteen Defilements of the Mind

"What, monks, are the defilements that defile the mind? Covetousness and unrighteous greed is a defilement that defiles the mind. Ill will . . . anger . . . hostility . . . denigration . . . insolence . . . envy . . . miserliness . . . deceit . . . fraud . . . obstinacy . . . rivalry . . . conceit . . . arrogance . . . vanity . . . heedlessness is a defilement that defiles the mind. Knowing that covetousness and unrighteous greed is a defilement that defiles the mind, a monk abandons it. Knowing that ill will . . . heedlessness is a defilement that defiles the mind, a monk abandons it."

(from MN 7, MLDB 118)

(2) Two Kinds of Thoughts

"Monks, before my enlightenment, while I was still an unenlightened bodhisatta, it occurred to me: 'Suppose that I divide my thoughts into two classes.' Then I set on one side thoughts of sensual desire, thoughts of ill will, and thoughts of harming, and I set on the other side thoughts of renunciation, thoughts of benevolence, and thoughts of harmlessness.

"As I dwelled thus, diligent, ardent, and resolute, a thought of sensual desire, a thought of ill will, or a thought of harming arose in me. I understood thus: 'This bad thought has arisen in me. This leads to my own affliction, to others' affliction, and to the affliction of both; it obstructs wisdom, causes difficulties, and leads away from nibbāna.' When I considered: 'This leads to my own affliction,' it subsided in me; when I considered: 'This leads to others' affliction,' it subsided in me; when I considered: 'This leads to the affliction of both,' it subsided in me; when I considered: 'This obstructs wisdom, causes difficulties, and leads away from nibbāna,' it subsided in me. Whenever a thought of sensual desire, a thought of ill will, or a thought of harming arose in me, I abandoned it, removed it, did away with it.

"Monks, whatever a monk frequently thinks and ponders upon, that will become the inclination of his mind. If he frequently thinks and ponders upon thoughts of sensual desire, he has abandoned the thought of renunciation to cultivate the thought of sensual desire, and then his mind inclines to thoughts of sensual desire. If he frequently thinks and ponders upon thoughts of ill will . . . thoughts of harming, he has abandoned the thought of harmlessness to cultivate the thought of harming, and then his mind inclines to thoughts of harming.

"Just as in the last month of the rainy season, in the autumn, when the crops thicken, a cowherd would guard his cows by constantly tapping and poking them on this side and that with a stick to check and curb them. Why is that? Because he sees that he could be flogged, imprisoned, fined, or blamed [if he let them stray into the crops]. So too I saw in unwholesome states danger, degradation, and defilement, and in wholesome states the blessing of renunciation, the aspect of cleansing.

"As I dwelled thus, diligent, ardent, and resolute, a thought of renunciation, a thought of benevolence, or a thought of harmlessness arose in me. I understood thus: 'This good thought has arisen in me. This does not lead to my own affliction, or to others' affliction, or to the affliction of both; it aids wisdom, does not cause difficulties, and leads to nibbāna. If I think and ponder upon this thought even for a night, even for a day, even for a night and day, I see nothing to fear from it. But with excessive thinking and pondering I might tire my body, and when the body is tired, the mind becomes disturbed, and when the mind is disturbed, it is far from concentration.' So I steadied my mind internally, quieted it, unified it, and concentrated it. Why is that? So that my mind should not be disturbed.

"Monks, whatever a monk frequently thinks and ponders upon, that will become the inclination of his mind. If he frequently thinks and ponders upon thoughts of renunciation, he has abandoned the thought of sensual desire to cultivate the thought of renunciation, and then his mind inclines to thoughts of renunciation. If he frequently thinks and ponders upon thoughts of benevolence . . . thoughts of harmlessness, he has abandoned the thought of harming to cultivate the thought of harmlessness, and then his mind inclines to thoughts of harmlessness.

"Just as in the last month of the hot season, when all the crops have been brought inside the village, a cowherd would guard his cows while staying at the root of a tree or out in the open, since he needs only to be mindful that the cows are there; so too, there was need for me only to be mindful that those states were there."

(from MN 19, MLDB 207–9)

(3) Practicing Effacement

The Blessed One said: "Now, Cunda, here effacement[5] should be practiced by you:

    (1) 'Others will inflict harm; we shall not inflict harm here': effacement should be practiced thus.

    (2) 'Others will destroy life; we shall abstain from the destruction of life here': effacement should be practiced thus.

    (3) 'Others will take what is not given; we shall abstain from taking what is not given here': effacement should be practiced thus.

    (4) 'Others will be uncelibate; we shall be celibate here': . . .

    (5) 'Others will speak falsehood; we shall abstain from false speech here': . . .

    (6) 'Others will speak divisively; we shall abstain from divisive speech here': . . .

    (7) 'Others will speak harshly; we shall abstain from harsh speech here': . . .

    (8) 'Others will indulge in idle chatter; we shall abstain from idle chatter here': . . .

    (9) 'Others will be covetous; we shall be uncovetous here': . . .

(10) 'Others will have ill will; we shall be benevolent here': ...

(11) 'Others will be of wrong view; we shall be of right view here': ...

(12) 'Others will be of wrong intention; we shall be of right intention here': ...

(13) 'Others will be of wrong speech; we shall be of right speech here':
...

(14) 'Others will be of wrong action; we shall be of right action here': ...

(15) 'Others will be of wrong livelihood; we shall be of right livelihood here': ...

(16) 'Others will be of wrong effort; we shall be of right effort here': ...

(17) 'Others will be of wrong mindfulness; we shall be of right mindfulness here': ...

(18) 'Others will be of wrong concentration; we shall be of right concentration here': ...

(19) 'Others will be of wrong knowledge; we shall be of right knowledge here': ...

(20) 'Others will be of wrong liberation; we shall be of right liberation here': ...

(21) 'Others will be overcome by dullness and drowsiness; we shall be free from dullness and drowsiness here': ...

(22) 'Others will be restless; we shall not be restless here': ...

(23) 'Others will be doubters; we shall go beyond doubt here': ...

(24) 'Others will be angry; we shall not be angry here': ...

(25) 'Others will be hostile; we shall not be hostile here': ...

(26) 'Others will be denigrators; we shall not be denigrators here': ...

(27) 'Others will be insolent; we shall not be insolent here': ...

(28) 'Others will be envious; we shall not be envious here': ...

(29) 'Others will be miserly; we shall not be miserly here': ...

(30) 'Others will be fraudulent; we shall not be fraudulent here': ...

(31) 'Others will be deceitful; we shall not be deceitful here': ...

(32) 'Others will be obstinate; we shall not be obstinate here': ...

(33) 'Others will be arrogant; we shall not be arrogant here': ...

(34) 'Others will be difficult to admonish; we shall be easy to admonish here': ...

(35) 'Others will have bad friends; we shall have good friends here': ...

(36) 'Others will be heedless; we shall be heedful here': ...

(37) 'Others will be faithless; we shall be faithful here': ...

(38) 'Others will be shameless; we shall be shameful here': ...

(39) 'Others will have no fear of wrongdoing; we shall be afraid of wrongdoing here': ...

(40) 'Others will be of little learning; we shall be of great learning here': ...

(41) 'Others will be lazy; we shall be energetic here': ...

(42) 'Others will be unmindful; we shall be mindful here': . . .

(43) 'Others will be foolish; we shall possess wisdom here': . . .

(44) 'Others will adhere to their own views, hold on to them tenaciously, and relinquish them with difficulty; we shall not adhere to our own views or hold on to them tenaciously, but shall relinquish them easily': effacement should be practiced thus."

(from MN 8, MLDB 125–27)

4. Loving-Kindness and Compassion

(1) The Four Divine Abodes

[The Buddha told the young brahmin Subha:][6] "Here a monk dwells pervading one quarter with a mind imbued with loving-kindness, likewise the second, likewise the third, likewise the fourth; so above, below, around, and everywhere and in every way, he dwells pervading the all-encompassing world with a mind imbued with loving-kindness, abundant, exalted, immeasurable, without hostility, and without ill will. When the liberation of mind by loving-kindness is developed in this way, no limiting kamma remains there, none persists there. Just as a vigorous trumpeter could make himself heard without difficulty in the four quarters, so too, when the liberation of mind by loving-kindness is developed in this way, no limiting kamma remains there,[7] none persists there. This is the path to the company of Brahmā.

"Again, a monk dwells pervading one quarter with a mind imbued with compassion . . . with a mind imbued with altruistic joy . . . with a mind imbued with equanimity, likewise the second, likewise the third, likewise the fourth; so above, below, around, and everywhere and in every way, he dwells pervading the all-encompassing world with a mind imbued with equanimity, abundant, exalted, immeasurable, without hostility, and without ill will. When the liberation of mind by equanimity is developed in this way, no limiting action remains there, none persists there. Just as a vigorous trumpeter could make himself heard without difficulty in the four quarters, so too, when the liberation of mind by equanimity is developed in this way, no limiting action remains there, none persists there."

(from MN 99, MLDB 816–17)

(2) Loving-Kindness Shines Like the Moon

"Monks, whatever grounds there are for making merit productive of a future birth, these do not equal a sixteenth part of the liberation of mind by loving-kindness. The liberation of mind by loving-kindness surpasses them and shines forth, bright and brilliant.

"Just as the radiance of all the stars does not equal a sixteenth part of the moon's radiance, but the moon's radiance surpasses them and shines forth, bright and brilliant, even so, whatever grounds there are for making merit productive of a future birth, these do not equal a sixteenth part of the liberation of mind by loving-kindness. The liberation of mind by loving-kindness surpasses them and shines forth, bright and brilliant.

"Just as in the last month of the rainy season, in the autumn, when the sky is clear and free of clouds, the sun, on ascending, dispels the darkness of space and shines forth, bright and brilliant, even so, whatever grounds there are for making merit productive of a future birth, these do not equal a sixteenth part of the liberation of mind by loving-kindness. The liberation of mind by loving-kindness surpasses them and shines forth, bright and brilliant.

"And just as in the night, at the moment of dawn, the morning star shines forth, bright and brilliant, even so, whatever grounds there are for making merit productive of a future birth, these do not equal a sixteenth part of the liberation of mind by loving-kindness. The liberation of mind by loving-kindness surpasses them and shines forth, bright and brilliant."

(It §27)

(3) The Benefits of Loving-Kindness

"Monks, when the liberation of the mind by loving-kindness has been pursued, developed, and cultivated, made a vehicle and basis, carried out, consolidated, and properly undertaken, eleven benefits are to be expected. What eleven? (1) One sleeps well; (2) one awakens happily; (3) one does not have bad dreams; (4) one is pleasing to human beings; (5) one is pleasing to spirits; (6) deities protect one; (7) fire, poison, and weapons do not injure one; (8) one's mind quickly becomes concentrated; (9) one's facial complexion is serene; (10) one dies unconfused; and (11) if one does not penetrate further, one fares on to the brahma world. When, monks, the liberation of the mind by loving-kindness has been repeatedly pursued, developed, and cultivated, made a vehicle and basis, carried out, consolidated, and properly undertaken, these eleven benefits are to be expected."

(AN 11:15, NDB 1573–74)

(4) Still More Benefits

"Monks, if someone were to give away a hundred pots of food as charity in the morning, at noon, and in the evening, and if someone else were to develop a mind of loving-kindness even for the time it takes to pull a cow's udder, either in the morning, at noon, or in the evening, this would be more fruitful than the former. Therefore, monks, you should train yourselves thus: 'We will develop and cultivate the liberation of mind by loving-kindness, make it our vehicle, make it our basis, stabilize it, exercise ourselves in it, and fully perfect it.' Thus should you train yourselves."

(SN 20:4, CDB 707)

(5) Loving-Kindness and Right Mindfulness

"'I will protect myself': thus should the establishments of mindfulness be practiced. 'I will protect others': thus should the establishments of mindfulness be practiced. Protecting oneself, one protects others; protecting others, one protects oneself.

"And how is it, monks, that by protecting oneself one protects others? By the pursuit, development, and cultivation [of the four establishments of mindfulness]. It is in such a way that by protecting oneself one protects others.

"And how is it, monks, that by protecting others one protects oneself? By patience, harmlessness, loving-kindness, and sympathy. It is in such a way that by protecting others one protects oneself.

"'I will protect myself': thus should the establishments of mindfulness be practiced. 'I will protect others': thus should the establishments of mindfulness be practiced. Protecting oneself, one protects others; protecting others, one protects oneself."

(from SN 47:19, CDB 1648–49)

(6) The Destruction of the Influxes

[The Venerable Ānanda is speaking to a householder named Dasama:] "Again, householder, a monk dwells pervading one quarter with a mind imbued with loving-kindness, likewise the second quarter, the third quarter, and the fourth quarter. Thus above, below, across, and everywhere and in every way, he dwells pervading the entire world with a mind imbued with loving-kindness, vast, exalted, measureless, without enmity, without ill will. He considers this and understands it thus: 'This liberation of the mind by loving-kindness is constructed and produced by volition. But whatever is constructed and produced by volition is impermanent, subject to cessation.' If he is firm in this, he attains the destruction of the influxes. But if he does not attain the destruction of the influxes because of that attachment to the Dhamma, because of that delight in the Dhamma, then, with the utter destruction of the five lower fetters, he becomes one of spontaneous birth, due to attain final nibbāna there without ever returning from that world."[8]

(from MN 52, MLDB 456; AN 11:16, NDB 1575)

III. Dealing with Anger

Introduction

Among the mental defilements disruptive to social harmony, probably the most pernicious is anger. Since virtually all communities, including Buddhist monasteries, consist of people still prone to egotistical desires, they are in constant danger of being riven by anger, resentment, and vindictiveness among their members. For this reason, the control of anger is critical to communal harmony. The Buddha recognizes that while giving vent to anger brings a certain degree of satisfaction, he points out that angry outbursts ultimately bounce back upon oneself, entailing direct harm for oneself and entangling one in conflict with others. Hence in **Text III,1** he describes anger as having "a poisoned root and honeyed tip."

Anger occurs in different degrees, which distinguish people into different types. **Text III,2** classifies people into three types on the basis of their relationship to anger: those who often get angry and nurture their anger are like a line etched in stone; those who often get angry but quickly dispel their anger are like a line drawn on the ground; those who remain patient even when attacked by others are like a line drawn in water. **Text III,3** further distinguishes people in relation to anger by comparing them to four kinds of vipers.

Since the Buddha seeks the solution to human problems with the aid of the principle of causality, to help us understand more clearly why anger arises, he lays out "ten grounds for resentment," which he enumerates in **Text III,4** with his customary thoroughness and precision. The ten are obtained by taking first one's reactions to those who act for one's own harm; next, one's reactions to those who act for the harm of one's friends; and next, one's reactions to those who act for the benefit of one's foes. Each of these is divided by way of the three periods of time—past, present, and future—for a total of nine. Finally, the Buddha adds irrational anger, the vexing case of "one who becomes angry without a reason."

The establishment of communal harmony requires that the members of the community strive to overcome anger. The first step in removing anger lies in reflecting on the dangers in anger. I have collated a number of discourses on the drawbacks of anger in **Texts III,5(1)–(4)**. Because anger poses such a formidable threat to one's well-being, the Buddha proposes a variety of methods for removing anger. In **Text III,6(1)** he teaches the ten occasions when resentment should be eliminated, counterparts to the ten grounds of resentment. Again, in **III,6(2)** he prescribes five methods to eliminate anger. In **Text III,6(3)**, the chief disciple Sāriputta explains another five methods to overcome anger.

Underlying the multiplicity of techniques to be deployed against anger stands one cardinal virtue, patience (*khanti*), which the Buddha calls the supreme austerity.[1] Patience is both the means for curing the mind of anger and the quality that prevails when anger has finally been subdued. In **Text III,7(1)** the Buddha instructs his disciples to remain patient when they are attacked by sharp words; even more, he says, "if bandits sever you savagely limb by limb with a two-handled saw," you are to restrain your wrath and extend to them a mind of loving-kindness. In **Text III,7(2)** Sāriputta teaches how a monk, when assailed by abusive words or attacked with weapons, can maintain patience by applying the contemplations of impermanence and the material elements. A discourse ascribed to Sakka, the ruler of the gods—included here as **Text III,7(3)**—contrasts two ways of dealing with transgression, that of the political realist and that of the ethical idealist. In this scenario, the celestial charioteer Mātali represents the political realist, who advocates punishment of enemies, while Sakka, as the righteous ruler, praises patience and restraint.

The challenge of maintaining patience can also be met by emulating worthy examples. In the last division of this part, therefore, I provide accounts of how exemplary figures upheld their commitment to patience under difficult circumstances. **Texts III,8(1)–(4)** show how the Buddha, the missionary monk Puṇṇa, the chief disciple Sāriputta, and the deity Sakka all drew upon patience to prevail over their adversaries.

III. Dealing with Anger

1. The Slaying of Anger

Sakka, ruler of the devas, approached the Blessed One, paid homage to him, stood to one side, and addressed the Blessed One in verse:

"Having slain what does one sleep soundly?
Having slain what does one not sorrow?
What is the one thing, O Gotama,
whose killing you approve?"

[The Blessed One:]

"Having slain anger, one sleeps soundly;
having slain anger, one does not sorrow.
The killing of anger, O Sakka,
with its poisoned root and honeyed tip:
this is the killing the noble ones praise,
for having slain that, one does not sorrow."

(SN 11:21, CDB 337)

2. Three Kinds of Persons

"Monks, there are these three kinds of persons found existing in the world. What three? The person who is like a line etched in stone; the person who is like a line etched in the ground; and the person who is like a line etched in water.

(1) "And what kind of person is like a line etched in stone? Here, some person often gets angry, and his anger persists for a long time. Just as a line etched in stone is not quickly erased by the wind and water but persists for a long time, so too, some person often gets angry, and his anger persists for a long time. This is called the person who is like a line etched in stone.

(2) "And what kind of person is like a line etched in the ground? Here, some person often gets angry, but his anger does not persist for a long time. Just as a line etched in the ground is quickly erased by the wind

and water and does not persist for a long time, so too, some person often gets angry, but his anger does not persist for a long time. This is called the person who is like a line etched in the ground.

(3) "And what kind of person is like a line etched in water? Here, some person, even when spoken to roughly and harshly, in disagreeable ways, remains on friendly terms with his antagonist, mingles with him, and greets him. Just as a line etched in water quickly disappears and does not persist for a long time, so too, some person, even when spoken to roughly and harshly, in disagreeable ways, remains on friendly terms with his antagonist, mingles with him, and greets him. This is called the person who is like a line etched in water.

"These, monks, are the three kinds of persons found existing in the world."

(AN 3:132, NDB 361–62)

3. Persons Like Vipers

"Monks, there are these four kinds of vipers. What four? The one whose venom is quick to come up but not virulent; the one whose venom is virulent but not quick to come up; the one whose venom is both quick to come up and virulent; and the one whose venom is neither quick to come up nor virulent. These are the four kinds of vipers. So too, there are these four kinds of persons similar to vipers found existing in the world. What four? The one whose venom is quick to come up but not virulent; the one whose venom is virulent but not quick to come up; the one whose venom is both quick to come up and virulent; and the one whose venom is neither quick to come up nor virulent.

(1) "And how, monks, is a person one whose venom is quick to come up but not virulent? Here, someone often becomes angry, but his anger does not linger for a long time. It is in this way that a person is one whose venom is quick to come up but not virulent. So, I say, this person is just like a viper whose venom is quick to come up but not virulent.

(2) "And how is a person one whose venom is virulent but not quick to come up? Here, someone does not often become angry, but his anger lingers for a long time. It is in this way that a person is one whose venom is virulent but not quick to come up. So, I say, this person is just like a viper whose venom is virulent but not quick to come up.

(3) "And how is a person one whose venom is both quick to come up and virulent? Here, someone often becomes angry, and his anger lingers for a long time. It is in this way that a person is one whose venom is both quick to come up and virulent. So, I say, this person is just like a viper whose venom is both quick to come up and virulent.

(4) "And how is a person one whose venom is neither quick to come up

nor virulent? Here, someone does not often become angry, and his anger does not linger for a long time. It is in this way that a person is one whose venom is neither quick to come up nor virulent. So, I say, this person is just like a viper whose venom is neither quick to come up nor virulent.

"These, monks, are the four kinds of persons similar to vipers found existing in the world."

(AN 4:110, NDB 491–92)

4. THE GROUNDS FOR RESENTMENT

"Monks, there are these ten grounds for resentment. What ten? (1) Thinking: 'They acted for my harm,' one harbors resentment. (2) Thinking: 'They are acting for my harm,' one harbors resentment. (3) Thinking: 'They will act for my harm,' one harbors resentment. (4) Thinking: 'They acted for the harm of one who is pleasing and agreeable to me,' one harbors resentment. (5) Thinking: 'They are acting for the harm of one who is pleasing and agreeable to me,' one harbors resentment. (6) Thinking: 'They will act for the harm of one who is pleasing and agreeable to me,' one harbors resentment. (7) Thinking: 'They acted for the benefit of one who is displeasing and disagreeable to me,' one harbors resentment. (8) Thinking: 'They are acting for the benefit of one who is displeasing and disagreeable to me,' one harbors resentment. (9) Thinking: 'They will act for the benefit of one who is displeasing and disagreeable to me,' one harbors resentment. (10) And one becomes angry without a reason. These, monks, are the ten bases of resentment."

(AN 10:79, NDB 1439)

5. DANGERS IN ANGER AND BENEFITS IN PATIENCE

(1) Five Dangers

"Monks, there are these five dangers in impatience. What five? One is displeasing and disagreeable to many people; one has an abundance of enmity; one has an abundance of faults; one dies confused; with the breakup of the body, after death, one is reborn in the plane of misery, in a bad destination, in the lower world, in hell. These are the five dangers in impatience.

"Monks, there are these five benefits in patience. What five? One is pleasing and agreeable to many people; one does not have an abundance of enmity; one does not have an abundance of faults; one dies unconfused; with the breakup of the body, after death, one is reborn in a good destination, in a heavenly world. These are the five benefits in patience."

(AN 5:215, NDB 825)

(2) Another Five Dangers

"Monks, there are these five dangers in impatience. What five? One is displeasing and disagreeable to many people; one is violent; one is remorseful; one dies confused; with the breakup of the body, after death, one is reborn in the plane of misery, in a bad destination, in the lower world, in hell. These are the five dangers in impatience.

"Monks, there are these five benefits in patience. What five? One is pleasing and agreeable to many people; one is not violent; one is without remorse; one dies unconfused; with the breakup of the body, after death, one is reborn in a good destination, in a heavenly world. These are the five benefits in patience."

(AN 5:216, NDB 825)

(3) Seven Dangers

"Monks, there are these seven things that are gratifying and advantageous to an enemy that come upon an angry man or woman. What seven?

(1) "Here, monks, an enemy wishes for an enemy: 'May he be ugly!' For what reason? An enemy does not delight in the beauty of an enemy. When an angry person is overcome and oppressed by anger, though he may be well bathed, well anointed, with trimmed hair and beard, dressed in white clothes, still, he is ugly. This is the first thing gratifying and advantageous to an enemy that comes upon an angry man or woman.

(2) "Again, an enemy wishes for an enemy: 'May he sleep badly!' For what reason? An enemy does not delight when an enemy sleeps well. When an angry person is overcome and oppressed by anger, though he may sleep on a couch spread with rugs, blankets, and covers, with an excellent covering of antelope hide, with a canopy and red bolsters at both ends, still, he sleeps badly. This is the second thing gratifying and advantageous to an enemy that comes upon an angry man or woman.

(3) "Again, an enemy wishes for an enemy: 'May he not succeed!' For what reason? An enemy does not delight in the success of an enemy. When an angry person is overcome and oppressed by anger, if he gets what is harmful, he thinks: 'I have gotten what is beneficial,' and if he gets what is beneficial, he thinks: 'I have gotten what is harmful.' When, overcome by anger, he gets these things which are diametrically opposed, they lead to his harm and suffering for a long time. This is the third thing gratifying and advantageous to an enemy that comes upon an angry man or woman.

(4) "Again, an enemy wishes for an enemy: 'May he not be wealthy!' For what reason? An enemy does not delight in the wealth of an enemy. When an angry person is overcome and oppressed by anger, kings appro-

priate for the royal treasury any wealth he has acquired by energetic striving, amassed by the strength of his arms, earned by the sweat of his brow, righteous wealth righteously gained. This is the fourth thing gratifying and advantageous to an enemy that comes upon an angry man or woman.

(5) "Again, an enemy wishes for an enemy: 'May he not be famous!' For what reason? An enemy does not delight in the fame of an enemy. When an angry person is overcome and oppressed by anger, he loses whatever fame he had acquired through heedfulness. This is the fifth thing gratifying and advantageous to an enemy that comes upon an angry man or woman.

(6) "Again, an enemy wishes for an enemy: 'May he have no friends!' For what reason? An enemy does not delight in an enemy having friends. When an angry person is overcome and oppressed by anger, his friends and companions, relatives, and family members avoid him from afar. This is the sixth thing gratifying and advantageous to an enemy that comes upon an angry man or woman.

(7) "Again, an enemy wishes for an enemy: 'With the breakup of the body, after death, may he be reborn in the plane of misery, in a bad destination, in the lower world, in hell!' For what reason? An enemy does not delight in an enemy's going to a good destination. When an angry person is overcome and oppressed by anger, he engages in misconduct by body, speech, and mind. As a consequence, still overcome by anger, with the breakup of the body, after death, he is reborn in the plane of misery, in a bad destination, in the lower world, in hell. This is the seventh thing gratifying and advantageous to an enemy that comes upon an angry man or woman.

"These are the seven things gratifying and advantageous to an enemy that come upon an angry man or woman."

(AN 7:64, NDB 1066–67)

(4) Being Spurned by Others

"What kind of person is to be looked upon with equanimity, not to be associated with, followed, and served? Here, some person is prone to anger and easily exasperated. Even if he is criticized slightly he loses his temper and becomes irritated, hostile, and stubborn; he displays irritation, hatred, and bitterness. Just as a festering sore, if struck by a stick or a shard, will discharge even more matter, so too . . . Just as a firebrand of the *tinduka* tree, if struck by a stick or shard, will sizzle and crackle even more, so too . . . Just as a pit of feces, if struck by a stick or a shard, becomes even more foul-smelling, so too some person here is prone to anger and . . . displays irritation, hatred, and bitterness. Such a person is to be looked upon with equanimity, not to be associated with, followed, and served. For what reason? [With the thought:] 'He might insult me, revile me, and do me harm.' Therefore such a person is to be looked upon with equanimity, not to be associated with, followed, and served."

(from AN 3:27, NDB 222)

6. REMOVING ANGER

(1) Ten Ways to Eliminate Resentment

"Monks, there are these ten ways of removing resentment. What ten? (1) Thinking: 'They acted for my harm, but what can be done about it?' one removes resentment. (2) Thinking: 'They are acting for my harm, but what can be done about it?' one removes resentment. (3) Thinking: 'They will act for my harm, but what can be done about it?' one removes resentment. (4) Thinking: 'They acted . . .' (5) . . . 'They are acting . . .' (6) . . . 'They will act for the harm of one who is pleasing and agreeable to me, but what can be done about it?' one removes resentment. (7) Thinking: 'They acted . . .' (8) . . . 'They are acting . . .' (9) . . . 'They will act for the benefit of one who is displeasing and disagreeable to me, but what can be done about it?' one removes resentment. (10) And one does not become angry without a reason. These, monks, are the ten ways of removing resentment."

(AN 10: 80, NDB 1440)

(2) The Buddha Teaches Five Ways

"Monks, there are these five ways of removing resentment by which a monk should entirely remove resentment when it has arisen toward anyone. What five? (1) One should develop loving-kindness for the person one resents; in this way one should remove the resentment toward that person. (2) One should develop compassion for the person one resents; in this way one should remove the resentment toward that person. (3) One should develop equanimity toward the person one resents; in this way one should remove the resentment toward that person. (4) One should disregard the person one resents and pay no attention to him; in this way one should remove the resentment toward that person. (5) One should apply the idea of the ownership of kamma to the person one resents, thus: 'This venerable one is the owner of his kamma, the heir of his kamma; he has kamma as his origin, kamma as his relative, kamma as his resort; he will be the heir of any kamma he does, good or bad.' In this way one should remove the resentment toward that person. These are the five ways of removing resentment by which a monk should entirely remove resentment when it has arisen toward anyone."

(AN 5:161, NDB 773–74)

(3) Sāriputta Teaches Five Ways

The Venerable Sāriputta addressed the monks: "Friends, there are these five ways of removing resentment by which a monk should entirely remove resentment when it has arisen toward anyone. What five? (1) Here, a person's bodily behavior is impure, but his verbal behavior is pure; one should remove resentment toward such a person. (2) A person's verbal behavior is impure, but his bodily behavior is pure; one should also remove resentment toward such a person. (3) A person's bodily behavior and verbal behavior are impure, but from time to time he gains an opening of the mind, placidity of mind; one should also remove resentment toward such a person. (4) A person's bodily behavior and verbal behavior are impure, and he does not gain an opening of the mind, placidity of mind, from time to time; one should also remove resentment toward such a person. (5) A person's bodily behavior and verbal behavior are pure, and from time to time he gains an opening of the mind, placidity of mind; one should also remove resentment toward such a person.

(1) "How, friends, should resentment be removed toward the person whose bodily behavior is impure but whose verbal behavior is pure? Suppose a rag-robed monk sees a rag by the roadside. He would press it down with his left foot, spread it out with his right foot, tear off an intact section, and take it away with him; so too, when a person's bodily behavior is impure but his verbal behavior is pure, on that occasion one should not attend to the impurity of his bodily behavior but should instead attend to the purity of his verbal behavior. In this way resentment toward that person should be removed.

(2) "How, friends, should resentment be removed toward the person whose verbal behavior is impure but whose bodily behavior is pure? Suppose there was a pond covered with algae and water plants. A man might arrive, afflicted and oppressed by the heat, weary, thirsty, and parched. He would plunge into the pond, sweep away the algae and water plants with his hands, drink from his cupped hands, and then leave; so too, when a person's verbal behavior is impure but his bodily behavior is pure, on that occasion one should not attend to the impurity of his verbal behavior but should instead attend to the purity of his bodily behavior. In this way resentment toward that person should be removed.

(3) "How, friends, should resentment be removed toward the person whose bodily behavior and verbal behavior are impure but who from time to time gains an opening of the mind, placidity of mind? Suppose there was a little water in a puddle. Then a person might arrive, afflicted and oppressed by the heat, weary, thirsty, and parched. He would think: 'This little bit of water is in the puddle. If I try to drink it with my cupped hands or a vessel, I will stir it up, disturb it, and make it undrinkable. Let me get

down on all fours, suck it up like a cow, and depart.' He then gets down on all fours, sucks the water up like a cow, and departs. So too, when a person's bodily behavior and verbal behavior are impure but from time to time he gains an opening of the mind, placidity of mind, on that occasion one should not attend to the impurity of his bodily and verbal behavior, but should instead attend to the opening of the mind, the placidity of mind, he gains from time to time. In this way resentment toward that person should be removed.

(4) "How, friends, should resentment be removed toward the person whose bodily and verbal behavior are impure and who does not gain an opening of the mind, placidity of mind, from time to time? Suppose a sick, afflicted, gravely ill person was traveling along a highway, and the last village behind him and the next village ahead of him were both far away. He would not obtain suitable food and medicine or a qualified attendant; he would not get to meet the leader of the village district. Another man traveling along the highway might see him and arouse sheer compassion, sympathy, and tender concern for him, thinking: 'Oh, may this man obtain suitable food, suitable medicine, and a qualified attendant! May he get to meet the leader of the village district! For what reason? So that this man does not encounter calamity and disaster right here.' So too, when a person's bodily and verbal behavior are impure and he does not gain from time to time an opening of the mind, placidity of mind, on that occasion one should arouse sheer compassion, sympathy, and tender concern for him, thinking, 'Oh, may this venerable one abandon bodily misbehavior and develop good bodily behavior; may he abandon verbal misbehavior and develop good verbal behavior; may he abandon mental misbehavior and develop good mental behavior! For what reason? So that, with the breakup of the body, after death, he will not be reborn in the plane of misery, in a bad destination, in the lower world, in hell.' In this way resentment toward that person should be removed.

(5) "How, friends, should resentment be removed toward the person whose bodily and verbal behavior are pure and who from time to time gains an opening of the mind, placidity of mind? Suppose there was a pond with clear, sweet, cool water, clean, with smooth banks, a delightful place shaded by various trees. Then a man might arrive, afflicted and oppressed by the heat, weary, thirsty, and parched. Having plunged into the pond, he would bathe and drink, and then, after coming out, he would sit or lie down in the shade of a tree right there. So too, when a person's bodily and verbal behavior are pure and from time to time he gains an opening of the mind, placidity of mind, on that occasion one should attend to his pure bodily behavior, to his pure verbal behavior, and to the opening of the mind, the placidity of mind, that he gains from time to time. In this way resentment toward that person should be removed. Friends, by

means of a person who inspires confidence in every way, the mind gains confidence.

"These, friends, are the five ways of removing resentment by means of which a monk can entirely remove resentment toward whomever it has arisen."

(AN 5:162, NDB 774–77)

7. Patience Under Provocation

(1) Being Patient When Criticized

"Monks, there are these five courses of speech that others may use when they address you: their speech may be timely or untimely, true or untrue, gentle or harsh, connected with good or with harm, spoken with a mind of loving-kindness or with inner hate. When others address you, their speech may be timely or untimely; when others address you, their speech may be true or untrue; when others address you, their speech may be gentle or harsh; when others address you, their speech may be connected with good or with harm; when others address you, their speech may be spoken with a mind of loving-kindness or with inner hate. Herein, monks, you should train thus: 'Our minds will remain unaffected, and we shall utter no evil words; we shall abide compassionate for their welfare, with a mind of loving-kindness, without inner hate. We shall abide pervading that person with a mind imbued with loving-kindness, and starting with him, we shall abide pervading the all-encompassing world with a mind imbued with loving-kindness, abundant, exalted, immeasurable, without hostility and without ill will.' That is how you should train, monks.

"Monks, suppose a man came with a hoe and a basket and said: 'I shall make this great earth to be without earth.' He would dig here and there, strew the soil here and there, spit here and there, and urinate here and there, saying: 'Be without earth, be without earth!' What do you think, monks? Could that man make this great earth to be without earth?" – "No, Bhante. Why is that? Because this great earth is deep and immense; it is not easy to make it be without earth. Eventually the man would reap only weariness and disappointment."

"So too, monks, there are these five courses of speech that others may use when they address you: their speech may be timely or untimely. . . . Herein, monks, you should train thus: 'Our minds will remain unaffected, and we shall utter no evil words; we shall abide compassionate for their welfare, with a mind of loving-kindness, without inner hate. We shall abide pervading that person with a mind imbued with loving-kindness; and starting with him, we shall abide pervading the all-encompassing world with a mind similar to the earth, abundant, exalted, immeasurable, without hostility and without ill will.' That is how you should train, monks.

"Monks, even if bandits were to sever you savagely limb by limb with a two-handled saw, he who gave rise to a mind of hate toward them would not be carrying out my teaching. Herein, monks, you should train thus: 'Our minds will remain unaffected, and we shall utter no evil words; we shall abide compassionate for their welfare, with a mind of loving-kindness, without inner hate. We shall abide pervading them with a mind imbued with loving-kindness; and starting with them, we shall abide pervading the all-encompassing world with a mind imbued with loving-kindness, abundant, exalted, immeasurable, without hostility and without ill will.' That is how you should train, monks."

(from MN 21, MLDB 221)

(2) Non-Retaliation

[The Venerable Sāriputta told the monks:] "So then, if others abuse, revile, scold, and harass a monk, he understands thus: 'This painful feeling born of ear-contact has arisen in me. That is dependent, not independent. Dependent on what? Dependent on contact.' Then he sees that contact is impermanent, that feeling is impermanent, that perception is impermanent, that volitional activities are impermanent, and that consciousness is impermanent. And his mind, having made an element its objective support, enters into [that new objective support] and acquires confidence, steadiness, and resolution.

"Now, if others attack that monk in ways that are unwished for, undesired, and disagreeable, by contact with fists, clods, sticks, or knives, he understands thus: 'This body is of such a nature that contact with fists, clods, sticks, and knives assail it. But this has been said by the Blessed One in his "advice on the simile of the saw": "Monks, even if bandits were to sever you savagely limb by limb with a two-handled saw, he who gave rise to a mind of hate toward them would not be carrying out my teaching." So tireless energy shall be aroused in me and unremitting mindfulness established, my body shall be tranquil and untroubled, my mind concentrated and unified. And now let contact with fists, clods, sticks, and knives assail this body; for this is just how the Buddha's teaching is practiced.'"

(from MN 28, MLDB 279–80)

(3) Patience Over Punishment

The Blessed One said this: "Once in the past, monks, the devas and the titans were arrayed for battle. Then Vepacitti, lord of the titans, addressed the titans thus: 'Dear sirs, in the impending battle between the devas and the titans, if the titans win and the devas are defeated, bind Sakka, lord of the devas, by his four limbs and neck and bring him to me in the city of the titans.' And Sakka, lord of the devas, addressed the devas thus: 'Dear sirs, in the impending battle between the devas and the titans, if the devas win and the titans are defeated, bind Vepacitti, lord of the titans, by his four limbs and neck and bring him to me in the Sudhamma assembly hall.'

"In that battle, monks, the devas won and the titans were defeated. Then the devas bound Vepacitti by his four limbs and neck and brought him to Sakka in their assembly hall. When Sakka was entering and leaving the assembly hall, Vepacitti, bound by his four limbs and neck, abused and reviled him with rude, harsh words. Mātali the charioteer addressed Sakka, lord of the devas, in verse:

> "'When face to face with Vepacitti
> is it, Sakka, from fear or weakness
> that you endure him so patiently,
> listening to his harsh words?'

[Sakka:]

> "'It is neither through fear nor weakness
> that I am patient with Vepacitti.
> how can a wise person like me
> engage in combat with a fool?'

[Mātali:]

> "'Fools would vent their anger even more
> if no one would keep them in check.
> hence with drastic punishment
> the wise man should restrain the fool.'

[Sakka:]

> "'I myself think this alone
> is the way to check the fool:
> when one knows one's foe is angry
> one mindfully maintains one's peace.'

[Mātali:]

> "'I see this fault, O Sakka,
> in practicing patient endurance:

when the fool thinks of you thus,
"He endures me out of fear,"
the dolt will chase you even more
as a bull does one who flees.'

[Sakka:]

"'Let it be whether or not he thinks,
"He endures me out of fear,"
of things that culminate in one's own good
none is found better than patience.

"'When a person endowed with strength
patiently endures a weakling,
they call that the supreme patience;
the weakling must be patient always.

"'They call that strength no strength at all—
the strength that is the strength of folly—
but no one can reproach a person
who is strong because guarded by Dhamma.

"'One who repays an angry man with anger
thereby makes things worse for himself.
Not repaying an angry man with anger,
one wins a battle hard to win.

"'He practices for the welfare of both—
his own and the other's—
when, knowing that his foe is angry,
he mindfully maintains his peace.

"'When he achieves the cure of both—
his own and the other's—
the people who consider him a fool
are unskilled in the Dhamma.'"

"So, monks, if Sakka, lord of the devas, could speak in praise of patience and gentleness, then how much more would it be fitting here for you, who have gone forth in such a well-expounded Dhamma and discipline, to be patient and gentle."

(SN 11:4, CDB 321–23)

8. Exemplars of Patience

(1) The Buddha Rejects Abuse

On one occasion the Blessed One was dwelling at Rājagaha in the Bamboo Grove, the Squirrel Sanctuary. The brahmin Akkosaka Bhāradvāja, Bhāradvāja the Abusive, heard: "It is said that another brahmin of the Bhāradvāja clan has gone forth from the household life into homelessness under the ascetic Gotama." Angry and displeased, he approached the Blessed One and abused and reviled him with rude, harsh words.

When he had finished speaking, the Blessed One said to him: "What do you think, brahmin? Do your friends and colleagues, kinsmen and relatives, as well as guests come to visit you?" – "They do, Master Gotama." – "Do you then offer them some food or a meal or a snack?" – "I do, Master Gotama." – "But if they do not accept it from you, then to whom does the food belong?" – "If they do not accept it from me, then the food still belongs to us."

"So too, brahmin, I do not abuse anyone, do not scold anyone, do not rail against anyone. I refuse to accept from you the abuse and scolding and tirade you let loose at me. It still belongs to you, brahmin! It still belongs to you, brahmin!

"Brahmin, one who abuses his own abuser, who scolds the one who scolds him, who rails against the one who rails at him—he is said to partake of the meal, to enter upon an exchange. But I do not partake of your meal; I do not enter upon an exchange. It still belongs to you, brahmin! It still belongs to you, brahmin!"

(SN 7:2, CDB 255–56)

(2) Puṇṇa's Courageous Spirit

[The Buddha said to the monk Puṇṇa:] "Now that I have given you this brief advice, in which country will you dwell?"

"Bhante, I am going to dwell in the Sunāparanta country."

"Puṇṇa, the people of Sunāparanta are fierce and rough. If they abuse and threaten you, what will you think then?"

"Bhante, if the people of Sunāparanta abuse and threaten me, then I shall think: 'These people of Sunāparanta are kind, truly kind, in that they did not give me a blow with the fist.' Then I shall think thus, Blessed One; then I shall think thus, Sublime One."

"But, Puṇṇa, if the people of Sunāparanta do give you a blow with the fist, what will you think then?"

"Bhante, if the people of Sunāparanta do give me a blow with the fist, then I shall think: 'These people of Sunāparanta are kind, truly kind, in that they did not give me a blow with a clod.' Then I shall think thus, Blessed One; then I shall think thus, Sublime One."

"But, Puṇṇa, if the people of Sunāparanta do give you a blow with a clod, what will you think then?"

"Bhante, if the people of Sunāparanta do give me a blow with a clod, then I shall think: 'These people of Sunāparanta are kind, truly kind, in that they did not give me a blow with a stick.' Then I shall think thus, Blessed One; then I shall think thus, Sublime One."

"But, Puṇṇa, if the people of Sunāparanta do give you a blow with a stick, what will you think then?"

"Bhante, if the people of Sunāparanta do give me a blow with a stick, then I shall think: 'These people of Sunāparanta are kind, truly kind, in that they did not give me a blow with a knife.' Then I shall think thus, Blessed One; then I shall think thus, Sublime One."

"But, Puṇṇa, if the people of Sunāparanta do give you a blow with a knife, what will you think then?"

"Bhante, if the people of Sunāparanta do give me a blow with a knife, then I shall think: 'These people of Sunāparanta are kind, truly kind, in that they have not taken my life with a sharp knife.' Then I shall think thus, Blessed One; then I shall think thus, Sublime One."

"But, Puṇṇa, if the people of Sunāparanta do take your life with a sharp knife, what will you think then?"

"Bhante, if the people of Sunāparanta do take my life with a sharp knife, then I shall think thus: 'There have been disciples of the Blessed One who, being humiliated and disgusted by the body and by life, sought to have their lives deprived by the knife. But I have had my life deprived by the knife without seeking for it.' Then I shall think thus, Blessed One; then I shall think thus, Sublime One."

"Good, good, Puṇṇa! Possessing such self-control and peacefulness, you will be able to dwell in the Sunāparanta country. Now, Puṇṇa, it is time to do as you think fit."

Then, having delighted and rejoiced in the Blessed One's words, the Venerable Puṇṇa rose from his seat, and after paying homage to the Blessed One, departed keeping him on his right. He then set his resting place in order, took his bowl and outer robe, and set out to wander toward the Sunāparanta country. Wandering by stages, he eventually arrived in the Sunāparanta country, and there he lived. Then, during that rains retreat, the Venerable Puṇṇa established five hundred men lay followers and five hundred women lay followers in the practice, and he himself realized the three clear knowledges.[2] On a later occasion, he attained final nibbāna.

(from MN 145, MLDB 1118–19)

(3) Sāriputta's Lion's Roar

On one occasion the Blessed One was dwelling at Sāvatthī in Jeta's Grove, Anāthapiṇḍika's Park. Then the Venerable Sāriputta approached the Blessed One and said to him: "Bhante, I have completed the rains residence at Sāvatthī. I want to make a tour of the countryside."

"You may go, Sāriputta, at your own convenience."

Then the Venerable Sāriputta rose from his seat, paid homage to the Blessed One, circumambulated him keeping the right side toward him, and departed. Then, not long after the Venerable Sāriputta had left, a certain monk said to the Blessed One: "Bhante, the Venerable Sāriputta struck me and then set out on tour without apologizing."

Then the Blessed One addressed a certain monk: "Go, monk, call Sāriputta.'"

"Yes, Bhante," that monk replied. Then he approached the Venerable Sāriputta and said: "The Teacher is calling you, friend Sāriputta."

"Yes, friend," the Venerable Sāriputta replied.

Now on that occasion the Venerable Mahāmoggallāna and the Venerable Ānanda took a key and wandered from dwelling to dwelling, calling out: "Come forth, venerables! Come forth, venerables! Now Sāriputta will roar his lion's roar in the presence of the Blessed One!"

Then the Venerable Sāriputta approached the Blessed One, paid homage to him, and sat down to one side. The Blessed One said to him: "Sāriputta, one of your fellow monks has complained that you struck him and then set out on tour without apologizing."

(1) "Bhante, one who has not established mindfulness of the body might strike a fellow monk and then set out on tour without apologizing. Just as they throw pure and impure things on the earth—feces, urine, spittle, pus, and blood—yet the earth is not repelled, humiliated, or disgusted because of this; so too, Bhante, I dwell with a mind like the earth, vast, exalted, and measureless, without enmity and ill will.

(2) "Bhante, one who has not established mindfulness of the body might strike a fellow monk and then set out on tour without apologizing. Just as they wash pure and impure things in water—feces, urine, spittle, pus, and blood—yet the water is not repelled, humiliated, or disgusted because of this; so too, Bhante, I dwell with a mind like water—vast, exalted, and measureless, without enmity and ill will.

(3) "Bhante, one who has not established mindfulness of the body might strike a fellow monk and then set out on tour without apologizing. Just as fire burns pure and impure things—feces, urine, spittle, pus, and blood—yet the fire is not repelled, humiliated, or disgusted because of this; so too, Bhante, I dwell with a mind like fire—vast, exalted, and measureless, without enmity and ill will.

(4) "Bhante, one who has not established mindfulness of the body might strike a fellow monk and then set out on tour without apologizing. Just as air blows upon pure and impure things—feces, urine, spittle, pus, and blood—yet the air is not repelled, humiliated, or disgusted because of this; so too, Bhante, I dwell with a mind like air—vast, exalted, and measureless, without enmity and ill will.

(5) "Bhante, one who has not established mindfulness of the body might strike a fellow monk and then set out on tour without apologizing. Just as a duster wipes off pure and impure things—feces, urine, spittle, pus, and blood—yet the duster is not repelled, humiliated, or disgusted because of this; so too, Bhante, I dwell with a mind like a duster—vast, exalted, and measureless, without enmity and ill will.

(6) "Bhante, one who has not established mindfulness of the body might strike a fellow monk and then set out on tour without apologizing. Just as an outcast boy or girl, clad in rags and holding a vessel, enters a village or town with a humble mind; so too, Bhante, I dwell with a mind like an outcast boy—vast, exalted, and measureless, without enmity and ill will.

(7) "Bhante, one who has not established mindfulness of the body might strike a fellow monk and then set out on tour without apologizing. Just as a bull with his horns cut, mild, well tamed and well trained, wanders from street to street and from square to square without hurting anyone with its feet or horns; so too, Bhante, I dwell with a mind like that of a bull with horns cut—vast, exalted, and measureless, without enmity and ill will.

(8) "Bhante, one who has not established mindfulness of the body might strike a fellow monk and then set out on tour without apologizing. Just as a young woman or man would be repelled, humiliated, and disgusted if the carcass of a snake, a dog, or a human being were slung around their neck; so too, Bhante, I am repelled, humiliated, and disgusted by this foul body.

(9) "Bhante, one who has not established mindfulness of the body might strike a fellow monk and then set out on tour without apologizing. Just as a person might carry around a cracked and perforated bowl of liquid fat that oozes and drips; so too, Bhante, I carry around this cracked and perforated body that oozes and drips.

"Bhante, one who has not established mindfulness of the body might strike a fellow monk here and then set out on tour without apologizing."

Then that accusing monk rose from his seat, arranged his upper robe over one shoulder, prostrated himself with his head at the Blessed One's feet, and said to the Blessed One: "Bhante, I have committed a transgression in that I so foolishly, stupidly, and unskillfully slandered the Venerable Sāriputta on baseless grounds. Bhante, may the Blessed One accept my transgression seen as a transgression for the sake of future restraint."

"Surely, monk, you have committed a transgression in that you so foolishly, stupidly, and unskillfully slandered the Venerable Sāriputta on baseless grounds. But since you see your transgression as a transgression and make amends for it in accordance with the Dhamma, we accept it. For it is growth in the Noble One's discipline that one sees one's transgression as a transgression, makes amends for it in accordance with the Dhamma, and undertakes future restraint."

The Blessed One then addressed the Venerable Sāriputta: "Sāriputta, pardon this hollow man before his head splits into seven pieces right there."

"I will pardon him, Bhante, if he asks me to pardon him."

(AN 9:11, NDB 1261–64)

(4) Sakka and the Anger-Eating Demon

The Blessed One said this: "Monks, once in the past a certain ugly deformed demon sat down on the seat of Sakka, ruler of the devas. Thereupon the devas found fault with this, grumbled, and complained about it, saying: 'It is wonderful indeed, sir! It is amazing indeed, sir! This ugly deformed demon has sat down on the seat of Sakka, ruler of the devas!' But to whatever extent the devas found fault with this, grumbled, and complained about it, to the same extent that demon became more and more handsome, more and more comely, more and more graceful.

"Then, monks, the devas approached Sakka and said to him: 'Here, dear sir, an ugly deformed demon has sat down on your seat. . . . But to whatever extent the devas found fault with this . . . that demon became more and more handsome, more and more comely, more and more graceful.' – 'That must be the anger-eating demon.'

"Then, monks, Sakka, ruler of the devas, approached that anger-eating demon, arranged his upper robe over one shoulder, and knelt down with his right knee on the ground. Then, raising his joined hands in reverential salutation toward that demon, he announced his name three times: 'I, dear sir, am Sakka, ruler of the devas! I, dear sir, am Sakka, ruler of the devas!' To whatever extent Sakka announced his name, to the same extent that demon became uglier and uglier and more and more deformed until he disappeared right there.

"Then, monks, having sat down on his own seat, instructing the devas, Sakka recited these verses:

> "'I am not one afflicted in mind,
> nor easily drawn by anger's whirl.
> I never become angry for long,
> nor does anger persist in me.

"'When I'm angry I don't speak harshly
and I don't praise my virtues.
I keep myself well restrained
out of regard for my own good.'"

(SN 11:22, CDB 338–39)

IV. Proper Speech

Introduction

One of the distinctive traits of human beings, which differentiates them from animals, is their capacity for speech. Words can create enmity or friendship, can win or harden hearts, can deceive others or open them to new pathways of understanding. Social transformations in the course of history have been facilitated by speech, whether spoken or written: just think of the impact of the Declaration of Independence, the Communist Manifesto, Lincoln's Gettysburg Address, and Martin Luther King's "I Have a Dream" speech. By means of speech new ideas are disseminated, new insights shared, and new horizons opened to human investigation. Speech has ignited wars and fostered peace. All the hopes and yearnings of the human heart, in every sphere of our collective existence, have found expression through the medium of speech.

In regard to the Dhamma, the role of speech is so important that the Buddha says one of the two conditions for the arising of right view is "the utterance of another."[1] Recognizing the pivotal role of speech, in both the noble eightfold path and among the ten courses of wholesome action he assigned four places to speech: abstaining from false speech, from divisive speech, from harsh speech, and from idle chatter—defined above in **Text II,2(5)**.

In Part IV, I expand on this earlier discussion by taking proper speech as a separate topic in its own right. The chapter begins with two short suttas on the constituents of "well-spoken speech"—**Texts IV,1(1)–(2)**—one enumerating four factors, the other five factors. Since the two do not completely correspond, the factors of well-spoken speech can be increased beyond the usual group of four. The Buddha also provides advice for those intent on holding discussions and participating in debates, which were commonplace among the contemporary ascetic and contemplative communities that flourished in northern India. These usually centered around a charismatic teacher. Adherents of rival sects would often meet to discuss and debate their respective tenets. Entire parks were set aside for wandering ascetics to dwell and discuss their views, and the larger towns featured a debating hall where ascetics would gather for debates.

While the Buddha tried to avoid fruitless debates conducted for the purpose of humiliating others and bolstering pride in one's own tenets, it was inevitable that as the monks wandered among the towns of northern India, they would be drawn into discussions with brahmins, philosophers, and ascetics of opposing views. In order to preserve the good repute of the Dhamma, they had to know how to engage in debate. One of the qualifications of the well-trained disciple was the ability to "explain their own teacher's doctrine, to teach it, proclaim it, establish it, disclose it, analyze it, and elucidate it, and to refute thoroughly with reasons the prevalent tenets of others and teach the efficacious Dhamma."[2] In **Text IV,2** the Buddha lays down standards for his own disciples to adopt when engaging in debates. He distinguishes among the different types of questions that might be asked, indicates how one should respond to these questions, and prescribes the attitudes one should bring into a debate. These are summed up in the concluding verses of this passage: the sagely person speaks without quarrelsomeness or pride, utters speech that the noble ones practice, and speaks in ways connected with the Dhamma and meaning.

One of the duties of a monk or nun was to teach and preach the Dhamma. To execute this duty effectively it was necessary to know how to address others in a way that would awaken their interest and hold their attention. Proficiency in teaching others might be seen as an aspect of "skill in means" (*upāyakosalla*). In **Text IV,3**, the Buddha explains five instances in which a talk is "wrongly addressed"—all cases when the subject of the talk does not match the temperament and interest of the audience. The "rightly addressed" talks are those whose subject matter matches the temperament and interest of the audience. These guidelines, however, should probably be seen as provisional strategies rather than as absolutes; for there are certainly cases when, for example, a talk on morality might be exactly what a dissolute person needs to hear, while a talk on generosity might be the most effective way to motivate a miser to undergo a change of heart and begin practicing charity.

Some texts included in this chapter may bring surprises. While the Buddha highlights the dangers in creating unnecessary arguments and in assigning praise and blame arbitrarily, without investigation—as is done respectively in **Texts IV,4** and **IV,5**—he does not insist that speech must always be sweet and agreeable to the hearers. To the contrary, he holds one should have no qualms about criticizing those who deserve criticism. Thus in **Text IV,6** he declares that one should speak praise and blame when they fit the situation, and in **IV,7** he even says that "when one knows overt sharp speech to be true, correct, and beneficial, one may utter it, knowing the time to do so."

Reproving others is a particularly thorny matter because of its potential to ignite resentment and sow the seeds of conflict. However, the moral mettle of any community depends on the upright conduct of its members, and thus when members stray beyond the bounds of propriety, it becomes obligatory to rein them in. In the Buddhist monastic order, to protect the integrity of the group, it is often necessary for one monk to reprove another. To maintain harmony and mutual respect during the process of reproach, in **Text IV,8**, Sāriputta describes the procedures to be followed by the person who intends to reprove another and the appropriate ways for the subject of reproach to respond to criticism. Thus while the discourses stress the importance of establishing a gentle and compassionate attitude before criticizing others, they do not advocate speaking to others only in agreeable ways. To the contrary, they advise one to censure others when criticism is due.

IV. Proper Speech

1. Well-Spoken Speech

(1) Possessing Four Factors

The Blessed One said this: "Monks, when speech possesses four factors, it is well spoken, not badly spoken, and it is blameless and irreproachable among the wise. What four? Here, a monk speaks only what is well spoken, not what is badly spoken. He speaks only Dhamma, not non-Dhamma. He speaks only what is pleasant, not what is unpleasant. He speaks only what is true, not lies. When speech possesses these four factors, it is well spoken, not badly spoken, and it is blameless and irreproachable among the wise."

(from Sn III,3; see too SN 8:5, CDB 284–85)

(2) Possessing Five Factors

"Monks, when speech possesses five factors, it is well spoken, not badly spoken, and it is blameless and irreproachable among the wise. What five? It is spoken at the proper time; what is said is true; it is spoken gently; what is said is beneficial; it is spoken with a mind of loving-kindness. When speech possesses these five factors, it is well spoken, not badly spoken, and it is blameless and irreproachable among the wise."

(AN 5:198, NDB 816)

2. Holding Discussions

"It is in relation to talk, monks, that a person may be understood as either fit to talk or unfit to talk. If this person is asked a question that should be answered categorically and he does not answer it categorically; if he is asked a question that should be answered after making a distinction and he answers it without making a distinction; if he is asked a question that should be answered with a counter-question and he answers it without asking a counter-question; if he is asked a question that should be set aside and he does not set it aside, in such a case this person is unfit to talk.[3]

"But if this person is asked a question that should be answered categorically and he answers it categorically; if he is asked a question that should be answered after making a distinction and he answers it after making a distinction; if he is asked a question that should be answered with a counter-question and he answers it with a counter-question; if he is asked a question that should be set aside and he sets it aside, in such a case this person is fit to talk.

"It is in relation to talk, monks, that a person should be understood as either fit to talk or unfit to talk. If this person is asked a question and he does not stand firm in regard to his position and the opposing position; if he does not stand firm in his stratagem; if he does not stand firm in an assertion about what is known; if he does not stand firm in the procedure, in such a case this person is unfit to talk.[4]

"But if this person is asked a question and he stands firm in regard to his position and the opposing position; if he stands firm in his stratagem; if he stands firm in an assertion about what is known; if he stands firm in the procedure, in such a case this person is fit to talk.

"It is in relation to talk, monks, that a person should be understood as either fit to talk or unfit to talk. If this person is asked a question and he answers evasively, diverts the discussion to an irrelevant subject, and displays anger, hatred, and bitterness, in such a case this person is unfit to talk.

"But if this person is asked a question and he does not answer evasively, divert the discussion to an irrelevant subject, or display anger, hatred, and bitterness, in such a case this person is fit to talk.

"It is in relation to talk, monks, that a person should be understood as either fit to talk or unfit to talk. If this person is asked a question and he overwhelms [the questioner], crushes him, ridicules him, and seizes upon a slight error,[5] in such a case this person is unfit to talk.

"But if this person is asked a question and he does not overwhelm [the questioner], or crush him, or ridicule him, or seize upon a slight error, in such a case this person is fit to talk.

"It is in relation to talk, monks, that a person should be understood as either having a supporting condition or not having a supporting condition. One who does not lend an ear does not have a supporting condition; one who lends an ear has a supporting condition. One who has a supporting condition directly knows one thing, fully understands one thing, abandons one thing, and realizes one thing. Directly knowing one thing, fully understanding one thing, abandoning one thing, and realizing one thing, he reaches right liberation.[6]

"This, monks, is the goal of talk, the goal of discussion, the goal of a supporting condition, the goal of lending an ear, that is, the emancipation of the mind through non-clinging."

Those who speak with quarrelsome intent,
settled in their opinions, swollen with pride,
ignoble, having assailed virtues,
look for openings to attack one another.

They mutually delight when their opponent
speaks badly and makes a mistake,
they rejoice in his bewilderment and defeat;
but noble ones don't engage in such talk.

If a wise person wants to talk,
having known the time is right,
without quarrelsomeness or pride,
the sagely person should utter
the speech that the noble ones practice,
which is connected with the Dhamma and meaning.

Not being insolent or aggressive,
with a mind not elated,
he speaks free from envy
on the basis of right knowledge.
He should approve of what is well expressed
but should not attack what is badly stated.

He should not train in fault-finding
nor seize on the other's mistakes;
he should not overwhelm and crush his opponent,
nor speak mendacious words.
Truly, a discussion among the good
is for the sake of knowledge and confidence.

Such is the way the noble discuss things;
this is the discussion of the noble ones.
Having understood this, the wise person
should not swell up but should discuss things.

(AN 3:67, NDB 287–89)

3. Speak in an Appropriate Way

"Monks, a talk is wrongly addressed when, having weighed one type of person against another, it is addressed to these five [inappropriate] types of persons. What five? A talk on faith is wrongly addressed to one devoid of faith; a talk on virtuous behavior is wrongly addressed to an immoral person; a talk on learning is wrongly addressed to one of little learning; a talk on generosity is wrongly addressed to a miser; a talk on wisdom is wrongly addressed to an unwise person.

(1) "And why is a talk on faith wrongly addressed to one devoid of faith? When a talk on faith is being given, a person devoid of faith loses his temper and becomes irritated, hostile, and stubborn; he displays anger, hatred, and bitterness. For what reason? Because he does not perceive that faith in himself and rejoice in it. Therefore a talk on faith is wrongly addressed to a person devoid of faith.

(2) "And why is a talk on virtuous behavior wrongly addressed to an immoral person? When a talk on virtuous behavior is being given, an immoral person loses his temper and becomes irritated, hostile, and stubborn; he displays anger, hatred, and bitterness. For what reason? Because he does not perceive that virtuous behavior in himself and rejoice in it. Therefore a talk on virtuous behavior is wrongly addressed to an immoral person.

(3) "And why is a talk on learning wrongly addressed to a person of little learning? When a talk on learning is being given, a person of little learning loses his temper and becomes irritated, hostile, and stubborn; he displays anger, hatred, and bitterness. For what reason? Because he does not perceive that learning in himself and rejoice in it. Therefore a talk on learning is wrongly addressed to a person of little learning.

(4) "And why is a talk on generosity wrongly addressed to a miser? When a talk on generosity is being given, a miser loses his temper and becomes irritated, hostile, and stubborn; he displays anger, hatred, and bitterness. For what reason? Because he does not perceive that generosity in himself and rejoice in it. Therefore a talk on generosity is wrongly addressed to a miser.

(5) "And why is a talk on wisdom wrongly addressed to an unwise person? When a talk on wisdom is being given, an unwise person loses his temper and becomes irritated, hostile, and stubborn; he displays anger, hatred, and bitterness. For what reason? Because he does not perceive that wisdom in himself and rejoice in it. Therefore a talk on wisdom is wrongly addressed to an unwise person.

"A talk is wrongly addressed when, having weighed one type of person against another, it is addressed to these five [inappropriate] types of persons.

"Monks, a talk is properly addressed when, having weighed one type of person against another, it is addressed to these five [appropriate] types of persons. What five? A talk on faith is properly addressed to one endowed with faith; a talk on virtuous behavior is properly addressed to a virtuous person; a talk on learning is properly addressed to a learned person; a talk on generosity is properly addressed to a generous person; a talk on wisdom is properly addressed to a wise person.

(1) "And why is a talk on faith properly addressed to one endowed with faith? When a talk on faith is being given, a person endowed with faith does not lose his temper and become irritated, hostile, and stubborn; he does not display anger, hatred, and bitterness. For what reason? Because he perceives that faith in himself and rejoices in it. Therefore a talk on faith is properly addressed to a person endowed with faith.

(2) "And why is a talk on virtuous behavior properly addressed to a virtuous person? When a talk on virtuous behavior is being given, a virtuous person does not lose his temper and become irritated, hostile, and stubborn; he does not display anger, hatred, and bitterness. For what reason? Because he perceives that virtuous behavior in himself and rejoices in it. Therefore a talk on virtuous behavior is properly addressed to a virtuous person.

(3) "And why is a talk on learning properly addressed to a learned person? When a talk on learning is being given, a learned person does not lose his temper and become irritated, hostile, and stubborn; he does not display anger, hatred, and bitterness. For what reason? Because he perceives that learning in himself and rejoices in it. Therefore a talk on learning is properly addressed to a learned person.

(4) "And why is a talk on generosity properly addressed to a generous person? When a talk on generosity is being given, a generous person does not lose his temper and become irritated, hostile, and stubborn; he does not display anger, hatred, and bitterness. For what reason? Because he perceives that generosity in himself and rejoices in it. Therefore a talk on generosity is properly addressed to a generous person.

(5) "And why is a talk on wisdom properly addressed to a wise person? When a talk on wisdom is being given, a wise person does not lose his temper and become irritated, hostile, and stubborn; he does not display anger, hatred, and bitterness. For what reason? Because he perceives that wisdom in himself and rejoices in it. Therefore a talk on wisdom is properly addressed to a wise person.

"Monks, a talk is properly addressed when, having weighed one type of person against another, it is addressed to these five [appropriate] types of persons."

(AN 5:157, NDB 770–72)

4. Don't Create Arguments

"Monks, when a monk is a maker of arguments, quarrels, disputes, contentious talk, and disciplinary issues in the Sangha, five dangers can be expected for him. What five? (1) He does not achieve what he has not yet achieved; (2) he falls away from what he has achieved; (3) a bad report circulates about him; (4) he dies confused; and (5) with the breakup of the body, after death, he is reborn in the plane of misery, in a bad destination, in the lower world, in hell. When a monk is a maker of arguments, quarrels, disputes, contentious talk, and disciplinary issues in the Sangha, these five dangers can be expected for him."

(AN 5:212, NDB 823)

5. Assigning Praise and Blame

"Monks, possessing five qualities, a resident monk is deposited in hell as if brought there. What five? (1) Without investigating and scrutinizing, he speaks praise of one who deserves dispraise. (2) Without investigating and scrutinizing, he speaks dispraise of one who deserves praise. (3) Without investigating and scrutinizing, he believes a matter that merits suspicion. (4) Without investigating and scrutinizing, he is suspicious about a matter that merits belief. (5) He squanders what has been given out of faith. Possessing these five qualities, a resident monk is deposited in hell as if brought there.

"Monks, possessing five qualities, a resident monk is deposited in heaven as if brought there. What five? (1) Having investigated and scrutinized, he speaks dispraise of one who deserves dispraise. (2) Having investigated and scrutinized, he speaks praise of one who deserves praise. (3) Having investigated and scrutinized, he is suspicious about a matter that merits suspicion. (4) Having investigated and scrutinized, he believes a matter that merits belief. (5) He does not squander what has been given out of faith. Possessing these five qualities, a resident monk is deposited in heaven as if brought there."

(AN 5:236, NDB 832–33)

6. Praise When Praise Is Due

Then the wanderer Potaliya approached the Blessed One and exchanged greetings with him. The Blessed One said to him: "Potaliya, there are these four kinds of persons found existing in the world. What four? (1) Here, some person speaks dispraise of someone who deserves dispraise, and the dispraise is accurate, truthful, and timely; but he does not speak praise of someone who deserves praise, though the praise would be accurate, truthful, and timely. (2) Some other person speaks praise of someone who deserves praise, and the praise is accurate, truthful, and timely; but he does not speak dispraise of someone who deserves dispraise, though the dispraise would be accurate, truthful, and timely. (3) Still another person does not speak dispraise of someone who deserves dispraise, though the dispraise would be accurate, truthful, and timely; and he does not speak praise of someone who deserves praise, though the praise would be accurate, truthful, and timely. (4) And still another person speaks dispraise of someone who deserves dispraise, and the dispraise is accurate, truthful, and timely; and he also speaks praise of someone who deserves praise, and the praise is accurate, truthful, and timely. These are the four kinds of persons found existing in the world. Now, Potaliya, which among these four kinds of persons seems to you the most excellent and sublime?"

"Of those four, Master Gotama, the one that seems to me the most excellent and sublime is the one who does not speak dispraise of someone who deserves dispraise, though the dispraise would be accurate, truthful, and timely; and who does not speak praise of someone who deserves praise, though the praise would be accurate, truthful, and timely. For what reason? Because what excels, Master Gotama, is equanimity."

"Of those four, Potaliya, the one that I consider the most excellent and sublime is the one who speaks dispraise of someone who deserves dispraise, and the dispraise is accurate, truthful, and timely; and who also speaks praise of someone who deserves praise, and the praise is accurate, truthful, and timely. For what reason? Because what excels, Potaliya, is knowledge of the proper time to speak in any particular case."

(AN 4:100, NDB 480–82)

7. Knowing What to Say and How to Say It

[The Buddha is speaking to the monks:] "It was said: 'One should not utter covert speech, and one should not utter overt sharp speech.' And with reference to what was this said?

"Here, monks, when one knows covert speech to be untrue, incorrect, and unbeneficial, one should not utter it. When one knows covert speech to be true, correct, and unbeneficial, one should try not to utter it. But when one knows covert speech to be true, correct, and beneficial, one may utter it, knowing the time to do so.

"Here, monks, when one knows overt sharp speech to be untrue, incorrect, and unbeneficial, one should not utter it. When one knows overt sharp speech to be true, correct, and unbeneficial, one should try not to utter it. But when one knows overt sharp speech to be true, correct, and beneficial, one may utter it, knowing the time to do so.

"So it was with reference to this that it was said: 'One should not utter covert speech, and one should not utter overt sharp speech.'"

(from MN 139, MLDB 1083–84)

8. Reproving Others

Venerable Sāriputta addressed the monks thus: "Friends, a monk who wishes to reprove another should first establish five things in himself. What five? (1) He should consider: 'I will speak at a proper time, not at an improper time; (2) I will speak truthfully, not falsely; (3) I will speak gently, not harshly; (4) I will speak in a beneficial way, not in a harmful way; (5) I will speak with a mind of loving-kindness, not while harboring hatred.' A monk who wishes to reprove another should first establish these five things in himself. . . .

"Friends, a person who is reproved should be established in two things: in truth and non-anger. He should reflect: 'If others should reprove me— whether at a proper time or at an improper time; whether about what is true or about what is false; whether gently or harshly; whether in a beneficial way or in a harmful way; whether with a mind of loving-kindness or while harboring hatred—I should still be established in two things: in truth and non-anger. If I know: "There is such a quality in me," I tell him: "It exists. This quality is found in me." If I know: "There is no such quality in me," I tell him: "It doesn't exist. This quality isn't found in me."' "

(from AN 5:167, NDB 780–82)

V. Good Friendship

Introduction

Strong communities depend on the personal relations between their members, and the most basic relation between people outside family connections is that of friendship. With Part V, as we move from personal cultivation, the focus of the previous chapters, to the establishment of interpersonal relations, we naturally begin with friendship. The Buddha placed special emphasis on one's choice of friends, which he saw as having a profound influence on one's individual development as well as on the creation of a harmonious and ethically upright community. Good friendship is essential not only because it benefits us in times of trouble, satisfies our social instincts, and enlarges our sphere of concern from the self to others. It is critical because good friendship plants in us *the sense of discretion*, the ability to distinguish between good and bad, right and wrong, and to choose the honorable over the expedient. Therefore the Buddha says that all other good qualities unfold from good friendship, and the popular Maṅgala Sutta, which enumerates thirty-two blessings, begins with "the avoidance of foolish persons and association with the wise."[1]

I start Part V with two short suttas—**Texts V,1(1)–(2)**—which enumerate the qualities of a good friend. The first is general, while the second is more specific to monastic life. **Text V,2** continues along the same track, but analyzes the qualities of a true friend in greater detail, distinguishing four types of "kind-hearted friends" and enumerating the distinctive qualities of each. **Text V,3** is extracted from a discourse addressed to a layman named Byagghapajja, who had inquired from the Buddha about things that "will lead to our welfare and happiness in this present life and in future lives." The Buddha responded by explaining four sources of benefit for a layperson in the present life: personal initiative, protection of one's wealth, good friendship, and balanced living. He followed this with four sources of benefit in future lives: faith, virtuous behavior, generosity, and wisdom. The friends with whom the layperson is advised to associate are those who exhort one in those same four qualities. Thus where the first, second, and fourth factors subsumed under temporal well-being are all concerned with ensuring one's economic security, good friendship is intended to establish a commitment to the values conducive to spiritual well-being. From this, it can be seen that while good friendship is listed under the factors pertaining to present welfare, on inspection it actually serves as a stimulus to spiritual development and thus becomes a bridge that connects temporal good in the present life with one's long-range well-being in lives to come.

Monastic life in Early Buddhism is sometimes imagined to be a solitary adventure in which the aspirant perpetually "dwells alone, withdrawn, diligent, ardent, and resolute."[2] There are indeed texts that convey such an impression. For instance, in verse after verse, the Khaggavisāṇa Sutta of the Suttanipāta enjoins the earnest seeker to forsake the crowd and "wander alone like the horn of a rhinoceros" (*eko care khaggavisāṇakappo*). Taken in isolation, these texts can be read as endorsing a highly individualistic version of monastic life in which all companionship is to be avoided. In actuality, however, just the opposite is the prevalent model. The Buddha created *a community* of men and women dedicated to the full-time practice of his teaching, and just as he advised laypeople to associate with good friends, he also instructed monastics to seek out good companions and guides in the spiritual life. He says that just as the dawn is the forerunner of the sunrise, so good friendship is the forerunner for the arising of the noble eightfold path, the "one thing very helpful for the arising of the noble eightfold path"; and, he adds, there is no other factor so conducive to the arising of the path as good friendship.[3]

In this section I have included two suttas that highlight the role of good friendship in the monastic life. In **Text V,4(1)**, when Ānanda comes to the Buddha and announces that good friendship is "half of the spiritual life," the Blessed One first restrains him and then corrects him by declaring that good friendship is "the entire spiritual life." And in **Text V,4(2)** he explains to the willful monk Meghiya four ways in which associating with good friends can bring to maturity the factors that ripen in liberation. The Vinaya shows how good friendship extends to the relationship between a preceptor and his pupils and between a teacher and his students. The Mahāvagga describes in vivid detail how teachers and students support one another and care for one another in living the spiritual life, but in this compilation I have limited my selections to texts from the corpus of suttas.[4]

V. Good Friendship

1. THE QUALITIES OF A TRUE FRIEND

(1) Seven Factors

"Monks, one should associate with a friend who possesses seven factors. What seven? (1) He gives what is hard to give. (2) He does what is hard to do. (3) He patiently endures what is hard to endure. (4) He reveals his secrets to you. (5) He preserves your secrets. (6) He does not forsake you when you are in trouble. (7) He does not roughly despise you. One should associate with a friend who possesses these seven factors."

> A friend gives what is hard to give,
> and he does what is hard to do.
> He forgives you your harsh words
> and endures what is hard to endure.
>
> He tells you his secrets,
> yet he preserves your secrets.
> He does not forsake you in difficulties,
> nor does he roughly despise you.
>
> The person here in whom
> these qualities are found is a friend.
> One desiring a friend
> should resort to such a person.

(AN 7:36, NDB 1021–22)

(2) Another Seven Factors

"Monks, one should associate with a monk friend who possesses seven qualities; one should resort to him and attend on him even if he dismisses you. What seven? (1) He is pleasing and agreeable; (2) he is respected and (3) esteemed; (4) he is a speaker; (5) he patiently endures being spoken to; (6) he gives deep talks; and (7) he does not enjoin one to do what is wrong."

He is dear, respected, and esteemed,
a speaker and one who endures speech;
he gives deep talks and does not enjoin one
to do what is wrong.

The person here in whom
these qualities are found is a friend,
benevolent and compassionate.
Even if one is dismissed by him,
one desiring a friend
should resort to such a person.

(AN 7:37, NDB 1022)

2. Four Kinds of Good Friends

[The Buddha is speaking to a young man named Sīgalaka:] "Young man, there are these four kinds of kind-hearted friends: the friend who is helpful; the friend who shares one's happiness and suffering; the friend who points out what is good; and the friend who is sympathetic.

"In four cases a helpful friend can be understood. He protects you when you are heedless; he looks after your property when you are heedless; he is a refuge when you are frightened; and when some need arises, he gives you twice the wealth required.

"In four cases a friend who shares one's happiness and suffering can be understood. He reveals his secrets to you; he guards your own secrets; he does not abandon you when you are in trouble; and he would even sacrifice his life for your sake.

"In four cases a friend who points out what is good can be understood. He restrains you from evil; he enjoins you in the good; he informs you of what you have not heard; and he points out to you the path to heaven.

"In four cases a sympathetic friend can be understood. He does not rejoice in your misfortune; he rejoices in your good fortune; he stops those who speak dispraise of you; and he commends those who speak praise of you."

(from DN 31, LDB 465–66)

3. Good Friendship in the Household Life

"What is good friendship? Here, in whatever village or town a clansman lives, he associates with householders or their sons—whether young and of mature virtue, or old and of mature virtue—who are accomplished in faith, virtuous behavior, generosity, and wisdom; he converses with them and engages in discussions with them. Insofar as they are accomplished in faith, he emulates them with respect to their faith; insofar as they are accomplished in virtuous behavior, he emulates them with respect to their virtuous behavior; insofar as they are accomplished in generosity, he emulates them with respect to their generosity; insofar as they are accomplished in wisdom, he emulates them with respect to their wisdom. This is called good friendship."

(from AN 8:54, NDB 1194–95)

4. Good Friendship in Monastic Life

(1) To Ānanda

Venerable Ānanda approached the Blessed One, paid homage to him, sat down to one side, and said: "Bhante, this is half of the spiritual life, that is, good friendship, good companionship, good comradeship."

"Not so, Ānanda! Not so, Ānanda! This is the entire spiritual life, Ānanda, that is, good friendship, good companionship, good comradeship. When a monk has a good friend, a good companion, a good comrade, it is to be expected that he will develop and cultivate the noble eightfold path.

"And how, Ānanda, does a monk with a good friend develop and cultivate the noble eightfold path? Here, a monk develops right view, which is based upon seclusion, dispassion, and cessation, maturing in release. He develops right intention . . . right speech . . . right action . . . right livelihood . . . right effort . . . right mindfulness . . . right concentration, which is based upon seclusion, dispassion, and cessation, maturing in release. It is in this way, Ānanda, that a monk with a good friend develops and cultivates the noble eightfold path.

"By the following method too, Ānanda, it may be understood how the entire spiritual life is good friendship, good companionship, good comradeship: by relying upon me as a good friend, beings subject to birth are freed from birth; beings subject to old age are freed from old age; beings subject to death are freed from death; beings subject to sorrow, lamentation, pain, dejection, and despair are freed from sorrow, lamentation, pain, dejection, and despair. By this method too, Ānanda, it may be understood how the entire spiritual life is good friendship, good companionship, good comradeship."

(SN 45:2, CDB 1524–25)

(2) When a Monk Has Good Friends

"Meghiya, when liberation of mind has not matured, five things lead to its maturation. What five? (1) Here, Meghiya, a monk has good friends, good companions, good comrades. When liberation of mind has not matured, this is the first thing that leads to its maturation. (2) Again, a monk is virtuous; he dwells restrained by the Pātimokkha,[5] possessed of good conduct and resort, seeing danger in minute faults. Having undertaken the training rules, he trains in them. When liberation of mind has not matured, this is the second thing that leads to its maturation. (3) Again, a monk gets to hear at will, without trouble or difficulty, talk concerned with the austere life that is conducive to opening up the heart. When liberation of mind has not matured, this is the third thing that leads to its maturation. (4) Again, a monk has aroused energy for abandoning unwholesome qualities and acquiring wholesome qualities; he is strong, firm in exertion, not casting off the duty of cultivating wholesome qualities. When liberation of mind has not matured, this is the fourth thing that leads to its maturation. (5) Again, a monk is wise; he possesses the wisdom that discerns arising and passing away, which is noble and penetrative and leads to the complete destruction of suffering. When liberation of mind has not matured, this is the fifth thing that leads to its maturation.

"When, Meghiya, a monk has good friends, good companions, good comrades, it can be expected of him that he will be virtuous, one who dwells restrained by the Pātimokkha; that he will get to hear at will, without trouble or difficulty, talk concerned with the austere life that is conducive to opening up the heart; that he will arouse energy for abandoning unwholesome qualities and cultivating wholesome qualities; that he will be wise, possessing the wisdom that discerns arising and passing away, which is noble and penetrative and leads to the complete destruction of suffering."

(from AN 9:3, NDB 1249–50; see too Ud 4.1)

VI. One's Own Good and the Good of Others

Introduction

In Part VI we move beyond binary friendships to see how the scriptures of Early Buddhism treat the relationship between the individual and those that come within his or her sphere of influence. Since the Buddha was primarily addressing monastics, the texts prioritize monastic concerns, but even these have wider implications. The first selection, **Text VI,1,** draws a contrast between the fool and the wise person, asserting that the fool—who is distinguished by bodily, verbal, and mental misconduct—is the cause of all calamities and misfortunes, while the wise person—distinguished by good conduct of body, speech, and mind—brings no calamity and misfortune. **Text VI,2** continues along the same track, but differentiates between the bad person and the good person on the basis of a larger set of criteria that explicitly refer to their respective impacts on others. The criteria comprise their dispositional qualities (which may be considered personal), their teachers and companions, their decisions, the way they counsel others, their speech, their action, their views, and their manner of giving.

Several earlier texts spoke of greed, hatred, and delusion as the roots of unwholesome action, and their opposites as the roots of wholesome action. In **Text VI,3**, in a conversation with a brahmin, the Buddha makes this correlation more specific. He explains that one overcome by greed, hatred, and delusion acts for his or her own affliction, the affliction of others, and the affliction of both, and again he states that such motivation underlies misconduct of body, speech, and mind. Moreover, one whose mind is overcome by these mental states cannot even distinguish what is good and what is bad, much less act appropriately. When they are abandoned, however, one can then make the necessary moral distinctions and act for the benefit of both oneself and others.

Text VI,4(1) distinguishes four kinds of persons on the basis of whether they are practicing (1) for their own welfare but not the welfare of others; (2) for the welfare of others but not their own welfare; (3) for the welfare of neither; and (4) for the welfare of both. The Buddha extols the one practicing for the welfare of both as "the foremost, the best, the preeminent, the supreme, and the finest of these four persons." It may seem strange that he ranks the one practicing for his own welfare but not the welfare of others over the one practicing for the welfare of others but not his own welfare, which seems directly contrary to some interpretations of the bodhisattva ideal. When, however, the intention is brought to light, the apparent contradiction vanishes.

The reason for this ranking emerges from **Texts VI,4(2)** and **VI,4(3)**, which elaborate on the four types of persons in relation to the removal of lust, hatred, and delusion and the observance of the five training rules. It turns out that the person who neglects his or her own welfare is one who makes no effort to overcome lust, hatred, and delusion and does not observe the five precepts. Since such a person will continue to act in the grip of the defilements and to engage in unwholesome actions, despite professed benevolent intentions, his or her deeds ultimately bring harm to others as well.

The next two sections in this chapter, **Texts VI,5** and **VI,6,** explain with reference to the monk and the lay follower, respectively, how one benefits oneself and others. Both sections relate the idea of "benefiting others" to instructing and guiding others in the Dhamma. Finally, in **Text VI,7,** the Buddha declares a person of great wisdom to be one who thinks of "his own welfare, the welfare of others, the welfare of both, and the welfare of the whole world." Discourses like this certainly show that an altruistic perspective was already integral to Early Buddhism, and that the Mahāyāna simply gave greater prominence to this attitude, perhaps in reaction to regressive tendencies that appeared among some of the schools that evolved out of the early teachings.

VI. One's Own Good
and the Good of Others

1. THE FOOL AND THE WISE PERSON

"Monks, one who possesses three qualities should be known as a fool. What three? Bodily misconduct, verbal misconduct, and mental misconduct. One who possesses these three qualities should be known as a fool. One who possesses three qualities should be known as a wise person. What three? Bodily good conduct, verbal good conduct, and mental good conduct. One who possesses these three qualities should be known as a wise person.

"Whatever perils arise, all arise on account of the fool, not on account of the wise person. Whatever calamities arise, all arise on account of the fool, not on account of the wise person. Whatever misfortunes arise, all arise on account of the fool, not on account of the wise person. Just as a fire that starts in a house made of reeds or grass burns down even a house with a peaked roof, plastered inside and out; so too, whatever perils arise . . . all arise on account of the fool, not on account of the wise person. Thus the fool brings peril, the wise person brings no peril; the fool brings calamity, the wise person brings no calamity; the fool brings misfortune, the wise person brings no misfortune. There is no peril from the wise person; there is no calamity from the wise person; there is no misfortune from the wise person.

"Therefore, monks, you should train yourselves thus: 'We will avoid the three qualities that make one known as a fool, and we will undertake and practice the three qualities that make one known as a wise person.' It is in this way that you should train yourselves."

(AN 3:1–2, NDB 201–2)

2. THE BAD PERSON AND THE GOOD PERSON

"Monks, a bad person is possessed of bad qualities; he associates as a bad person, he decides as a bad person, he counsels as a bad person, he speaks as a bad person, he acts as a bad person, he holds views as a bad person, and he gives gifts as a bad person.

"And how is a bad person possessed of bad qualities? Here a bad person has no faith, no shame, no fear of wrongdoing; he is unlearned, lazy, forgetful, and unwise. That is how a bad person is possessed of bad qualities.

"And how does a bad person associate as a bad person? Here a bad person has for friends and companions those ascetics and brahmins who have no faith, no shame, no fear of wrongdoing; who are unlearned, lazy, forgetful, and unwise. That is how a bad person associates as a bad person.

"And how does a bad person decide as a bad person? Here a bad person decides for his own affliction, for the affliction of others, and for the affliction of both. That is how a bad person decides as a bad person.

"And how does a bad person counsel as a bad person? Here a bad person counsels for his own affliction, for the affliction of others, and for the affliction of both. That is how a bad person counsels as a bad person.

"And how does a bad person speak as a bad person? Here a bad person speaks false speech, divisive speech, harsh speech, and idle chatter. That is how a bad person speaks as a bad person.

"And how does a bad person act as a bad person? Here a bad person destroys life, takes what is not given, and engages in sexual misconduct. That is how a bad person acts as a bad person.

"And how does a bad person hold views as a bad person? Here a bad person holds such a view as this: 'There is nothing given, nothing offered, nothing sacrificed; no fruit or result of good and bad actions; no this world, no other world; no mother, no father; no beings who are reborn spontaneously; no good and virtuous ascetics and brahmins in the world who have realized for themselves by direct knowledge and declare this world and the other world.' That is how a bad person holds views as a bad person.

"And how does a bad person give gifts as a bad person? Here a bad person gives a gift carelessly, gives it not with his own hand, gives it without showing respect, gives what is to be discarded, gives it with the view that nothing will come of it. That is how a bad person gives gifts as a bad person.

"That bad person—thus possessed of bad qualities, who thus associates as a bad person, decides as a bad person, counsels as a bad person, speaks as a bad person, acts as a bad person, holds views as a bad person, and gives gifts as a bad person—on the dissolution of the body, after death, is reborn in the destination of bad people. And what is the destination of bad people? It is hell or the animal world. . . .

"Monks, a good person is possessed of good qualities; he associates as a good person, he decides as a good person, he counsels as a good person, he speaks as a good person, he acts as a good person, he holds views as a good person, and he gives gifts as a good person.

"And how is a good person possessed of good qualities? Here a good person has faith, shame, and fear of wrongdoing; he is learned, energetic, mindful, and wise. That is how a good person is possessed of good qualities.

"And how does a good person associate as a good person? Here a good person has for his friends and companions those ascetics and brahmins who have faith, shame, and fear of wrongdoing; who are learned, energetic, mindful, and wise. That is how a good person associates as a good person.

"And how does a good person decide as a good person? Here a good person does not decide for his own affliction, for the affliction of others, or for the affliction of both. That is how a good person decides as a good person.

"And how does a good person counsel as a good person? Here a good person does not counsel for his own affliction, for the affliction of others, or for the affliction of both. That is how a good person counsels as a good person.

"And how does a good person speak as a good person? Here a good person abstains from false speech, from divisive speech, from harsh speech, and from idle chatter. That is how a good person speaks as a good person.

"And how does a good person act as a good person? Here a good person abstains from the destruction of life, from taking what is not given, and from sexual misconduct. That is how a good person acts as a good person.

"And how does a good person hold views as a good person? Here a good person holds such a view as this: 'There is what is given, offered, and sacrificed; there is fruit and result of good and bad actions; there is this world and the other world; there is mother and father; there are beings who are reborn spontaneously; there are good and virtuous ascetics and brahmins in the world who have realized for themselves by direct knowledge and declare this world and the other world.' That is how a good person holds views as a good person.

"And how does a good person give gifts as a good person? Here a good person gives a gift carefully, gives it with his own hand, gives it showing respect, gives a valuable gift, gives it with the view that something will come of it. That is how a good person gives gifts as a good person.

"That good person—thus possessed of good qualities, who thus associates as a good person, decides as a good person, counsels as a good person, speaks as a good person, acts as a good person, holds views as a good person, and gives gifts as a good person—on the dissolution of the body, after death, is reborn in the destination of good people. And what is the destination of good people? It is greatness among the devas or human beings."

(from MN 110, MLDB 892–95)

3. The Roots of Harm and Benefit for Self and Others

A certain brahmin wanderer approached the Blessed One and said to him: "Master Gotama, it is said: 'A directly visible Dhamma, a directly visible Dhamma.' In what way is the Dhamma directly visible, immediate, inviting one to come and see, applicable, to be personally experienced by the wise?"

(1) "Brahmin, one overcome by greed intends for his own affliction, for the affliction of others, or for the affliction of both, and he experiences mental suffering and dejection. But when greed is abandoned, he does not intend for his own affliction, for the affliction of others, or for the affliction of both, and he does not experience mental suffering and dejection. One overcome by greed engages in misconduct by body, speech, and mind. But when greed is abandoned, he does not engage in misconduct by body, speech, and mind. One overcome by greed does not understand as it really is his own good, the good of others, or the good of both. But when greed is abandoned, he understands as it really is his own good, the good of others, and the good of both. It is in this way, brahmin, that the Dhamma is directly visible . . . to be personally experienced by the wise.

(2) "Brahmin, one overcome by hatred intends for his own affliction, for the affliction of others, or for the affliction of both, and he experiences mental suffering and dejection. But when hatred is abandoned, he does not intend for his own affliction, for the affliction of others, or for the affliction of both, and he does not experience mental suffering and dejection. One overcome by hatred engages in misconduct by body, speech, and mind. But when hatred is abandoned, he does not engage in misconduct by body, speech, and mind. One overcome by hatred does not understand as it really is his own good, the good of others, or the good of both. But when hatred is abandoned, he understands as it really is his own good, the good of others, and the good of both. It is in this way, brahmin, that the Dhamma is directly visible . . . to be personally experienced by the wise.

(3) "One overcome by delusion intends for his own affliction, for the affliction of others, or for the affliction of both, and he experiences mental suffering and dejection. But when delusion is abandoned, he does not intend for his own affliction, for the affliction of others, or for the affliction of both, and he does not experience mental suffering and dejection. One overcome by delusion engages in misconduct by body, speech, and mind. But when delusion is abandoned, he does not engage in misconduct by body, speech, and mind. One overcome by delusion does not understand as it really is his own good, the good of others, or the good of both. But when delusion is abandoned, he understands as it really is his own good,

the good of others, and the good of both. It is in this way, too, that the Dhamma is directly visible, immediate, inviting one to come and see, applicable, to be personally experienced by the wise."

(AN 3:54, NDB 250–51)

4. Four Kinds of Persons in the World

(1) The Best Kind of Person

"Monks, there are these four kinds of persons found existing in the world. What four? (1) One who is practicing neither for his own welfare nor for the welfare of others; (2) one who is practicing for the welfare of others but not for his own welfare; (3) one who is practicing for his own welfare but not for the welfare of others; and (4) one who is practicing both for his own welfare and for the welfare of others.

"Suppose a cremation brand was blazing at both ends and smeared with dung in the middle: it could not be used as timber either in the village or in the forest. Just like this, I say, is the person who is practicing neither for his own welfare nor for the welfare of others.

"Monks, the person among these who is practicing for the welfare of others but not for his own welfare is the more excellent and sublime of the [first] two persons. The person practicing for his own welfare but not for the welfare of others is the more excellent and sublime of the [first] three persons. The person practicing both for his own welfare and for the welfare of others is the foremost, the best, the preeminent, the supreme, and the finest of these four persons. Just as from a cow comes milk, from milk curd, from curd butter, from butter ghee, and from ghee comes cream-of-ghee, which is reckoned the foremost of all these, so the person practicing both for his own welfare and for the welfare of others is the foremost, the best, the preeminent, the supreme, and the finest of these four persons.

"These are the four kinds of persons found existing in the world."

(AN 4:95, NDB 476–77)

(2) The Removal of Lust, Hatred, and Delusion

"Monks, there are these four kinds of persons found existing in the world. What four? (1) One who is practicing for his own welfare but not for the welfare of others; (2) one who is practicing for the welfare of others but not for his own welfare; (3) one who is practicing neither for his own welfare nor for the welfare of others; and (4) one who is practicing both for his own welfare and for the welfare of others.

(1) "And how is a person practicing for his own welfare but not for the

welfare of others? Here, some person practices to remove his own lust, hatred, and delusion but does not encourage others to remove their lust, hatred, and delusion. It is in this way that a person is practicing for his own welfare but not for the welfare of others.

(2) "And how is a person practicing for the welfare of others but not for his own welfare? Here, some person encourages others to remove their lust, hatred, and delusion, but does not practice to remove his own lust, hatred, and delusion. It is in this way that a person is practicing for the welfare of others but not for his own welfare.

(3) "And how is a person practicing neither for his own welfare nor for the welfare of others? Here, some person does not practice to remove his own lust, hatred, and delusion, nor does he encourage others to remove their lust, hatred, and delusion. It is in this way that a person is practicing neither for his own welfare nor for the welfare of others.

(4) "And how is a person practicing both for his own welfare and for the welfare of others? Here, some person practices to remove his own lust, hatred, and delusion, and he encourages others to remove their lust, hatred, and delusion. It is in this way that a person is practicing both for his own welfare and for the welfare of others.

"These, monks, are the four kinds of persons found existing in the world."

(AN 4:96, NDB 477–78)

(3) The Five Training Rules

"Monks, there are these four kinds of persons found existing in the world. What four? (1) One who is practicing for his own welfare but not for the welfare of others; (2) one who is practicing for the welfare of others but not for his own welfare; (3) one who is practicing neither for his own welfare nor for the welfare of others; and (4) one who is practicing both for his own welfare and for the welfare of others.

(1) "And how is a person practicing for his own welfare but not for the welfare of others? Here, some person himself abstains from the destruction of life but does not encourage others to abstain from the destruction of life. He himself abstains from taking what is not given but does not encourage others to abstain from taking what is not given. He himself abstains from sexual misconduct but does not encourage others to abstain from sexual misconduct. He himself abstains from false speech but does not encourage others to abstain from false speech. He himself abstains from liquor, wine, and intoxicants, but does not encourage others to abstain from them. It is in this way that a person is practicing for his own welfare but not for the welfare of others.

(2) "And how is a person practicing for the welfare of others but not for

his own welfare? Here, some person does not himself abstain from the destruction of life but he encourages others to abstain from the destruction of life. . . . He does not himself abstain from liquor, wine, and intoxicants, but he encourages others to abstain from them. It is in this way that a person is practicing for the welfare of others but not for his own welfare.

(3) "And how is a person practicing neither for his own welfare nor for the welfare of others? Here, some person does not himself abstain from the destruction of life and does not encourage others to abstain from the destruction of life. . . . He does not himself abstain from liquor, wine, and intoxicants, and does not encourage others to abstain from them. It is in this way that a person is practicing neither for his own welfare nor for the welfare of others.

(4) "And how is a person practicing both for his own welfare and for the welfare of others? Here, some person himself abstains from the destruction of life and encourages others to abstain from the destruction of life. . . . He himself abstains from liquor, wine, and intoxicants, and encourages others to abstain from them. It is in this way that he is practicing both for his own welfare and for the welfare of others.

"These, monks, are the four kinds of persons found existing in the world."

(AN 4:99, NDB 479–80)

5. The Monk

"Monks, possessing five qualities, a monk is practicing both for his own welfare and for the welfare of others. What five? (1) Here, a monk is himself accomplished in virtuous behavior and encourages others to become accomplished in virtuous behavior; (2) he is himself accomplished in concentration and encourages others to become accomplished in concentration; (3) he is himself accomplished in wisdom and encourages others to become accomplished in wisdom; (4) he is himself accomplished in liberation and encourages others to become accomplished in liberation; (5) he is himself accomplished in the knowledge and vision of liberation and encourages others to become accomplished in the knowledge and vision of liberation. Possessing these five qualities, a monk is practicing both for his own welfare and for the welfare of others."

(AN 5:20, NDB 639–40)

6. The Lay Follower

Mahānāma the Sakyan asked the Blessed One: "In what way, Bhante, is a lay follower practicing for his own welfare and for the welfare of others?"

(1) "When, Mahānāma, a lay follower is himself accomplished in faith

and also encourages others to accomplish faith; (2) he is himself accomplished in virtuous behavior and also encourages others to accomplish virtuous behavior; (3) he is himself accomplished in generosity and also encourages others to accomplish generosity; (4) he himself wants to see monks and also encourages others to see monks; (5) he himself wants to hear the good Dhamma and also encourages others to hear the good Dhamma; (6) he himself retains in mind the teachings he has heard and also encourages others to retain the teachings in mind; (7) he himself examines the meaning of the teachings that have been retained in mind and also encourages others to examine their meaning; (8) he himself understands the meaning and the Dhamma and then practices in accordance with the Dhamma, and also encourages others to practice in accordance with the Dhamma. It is in this way, Mahānāma, that a lay follower is practicing for his own welfare and also for the welfare of others."

(from AN 8:25, NDB 1155)

7. One of Great Wisdom

A certain monk asked the Blessed One: "It is said, Bhante, 'a wise person of great wisdom, a wise person of great wisdom.' In what way is one a wise person of great wisdom?"

"Here, monk, a wise person of great wisdom does not intend for his own affliction, or for the affliction of others, or for the affliction of both. Rather, when he plans, he plans for his own welfare, the welfare of others, the welfare of both, and the welfare of the whole world. It is in this way that one is a wise person of great wisdom."

(from AN 4:186, NDB 555)

VII. The Intentional Community

Introduction

Communities can be distinguished into two types, which we might call the natural and the intentional. A natural community is one that emerges spontaneously from the natural bonds between people. In concrete experience the natural community is already given along with the lifeworld in which we are embedded. We do not form natural communities but find ourselves immersed in them, even from birth, as completely as a fish is immersed in the sea. Our lives are thoroughly interwoven with the natural community, from which we can never be separated; only a floating and porous boundary separates the personal self and the natural community. Intentional communities, in contrast, are formed deliberately. They bring people together under the banner of a shared purpose or common ideals. They usually set up qualifications for membership and are governed by rules and regulations. They are subject to fissures and must ensure that their members remain loyal to the purpose of the group and behave in ways that support its success. Such communities usually also set up boundaries the transgression of which entails expulsion from their ranks.

The principles that govern an intentional community were of particular concern to the Buddha because he was the founder of a monastic order that brought together men and women under a shared commitment to this teaching. The members of the order came from different geographical areas, had been born into different castes, had very different ideas and attitudes, and even spoke different dialects. He was also the guide to a still larger congregation of lay followers spread out over an area that extended roughly from present-day Delhi to West Bengal. Thus for the Buddha, maintaining the cohesiveness of his community was a critical task, constantly being challenged by the tensions in communal living. He foresaw that to ensure that his teaching survived intact, it was necessary to lay down rules that would prescribe uniform standards of behavior and define the procedures for conducting communal affairs. In the face of divisive pressures and even rebellion, he had to preserve harmony and heal conflicts, which erupted several times in the course of his teaching career.

Part VII consists of texts that pertain to the establishment and maintenance of the intentional community. While most of the texts chosen make particular reference to the monastic order, the purposes behind these principles are not necessarily tied to a monastic regimen. The principles they propose can be adopted by other communities and modified in accordance with their aims.

The chapter begins with a series of short discourses, **Texts VII,1(1)–(5)**, that distinguish five opposite kinds of communities—the shallow and the deep, the divided and the harmonious, and so forth—extolling the worthy types of community over the unworthy types.[1] **Texts VII,2(1)–(3)** discuss the forces of attraction that draw people together into communities. The general factor is stated in **VII,2(1)**: people meet and unite "by way of elements." On account of their disposition (*adhimutti*), people unite with those who share their interests and aims. The forces of attraction again divide the resultant communities into two types: the bad union, which is like excrement merging with excrement or spittle with spittle, and the good union, which is like milk merging with milk or honey with honey. **Text VII,2(2)** chains together a number of discourses that specify the "elements" on account of which people unite, mentioning both the bad qualities and the good qualities that bring people together. In still another discourse not included here (SN 14:15), the Buddha points out how monks inclined to wisdom gather around Sāriputta; those inclined to psychic powers gather around Moggallāna; those interested in monastic discipline gather around Upāli; those disposed to the austere practices gather around Mahākassapa; and those of evil desires congregate around Devadatta, the Buddha's ambitious cousin.

One set of principles for building a healthy community is the four *saṅgahavatthu*, a term that might be translated as the "four means of embracing others" or the "four means of attraction and support." These were initially prescribed as methods by which an individual could build up a network of friendships, but they can also be utilized to create and maintain harmonious relationships within a larger group. The four— sketched in **Text VII,2(3)**—are giving, endearing speech, beneficient conduct, and impartiality, the last interpreted to mean the treatment of others as equal to oneself. This particular set, strangely, is mentioned only on a few occasions in the scriptures of Early Buddhism. They receive much more attention in the Mahāyāna sūtras and treatises, where they are listed as one of the chief means that a bodhisattva employs to attract others and transform them in a positive direction.

Once an intentional community has taken shape, critical to its success is the issue of leadership. During the Buddha's own lifetime, his followers always looked to him as the standard of authority and thus his personal charisma was sufficient for the disciples to accept his injunctions as binding. But before his passing, the Buddha refused to appoint a personal successor, instead urging his disciples to regard the Dhamma and the

Vinaya as their teacher and standard of authority: "It may be, Ānanda, that you think: 'The teaching has lost its teacher. We no longer have a teacher.' You should not think in such a way. The Dhamma and Vinaya taught and promulgated by me will be your teacher after I am gone."[2] **Text VII,3(1)** enunciates the same principle. The Venerable Ānanda is asked by the brahmin Vassakāra, chief minister of Magadha, how the monks remain cohesive when their teacher has passed away. Ānanda replies that even though the Buddha is gone, they are not without a refuge, for they still have the Dhamma as their refuge.

As a legislator for his community, the Buddha laid down a detailed set of rules for the monks and nuns, which are minutely described and defined in the Vinaya Piṭaka. The training rules were also intended to promote concord and harmony, both among monastics and between the monastics and the lay community. This can be seen in **Text VII,3(2)**, which enumerates the ten reasons the Buddha promulgates a training rule. Two among the ten reasons show that the rules were partly laid down to inspire faith in those householders without faith in the teaching and to strengthen the faith of those lay devotees who had already accepted the Dhamma.

The Vinaya Piṭaka contains not only explanations of the individual monastic rules but also the regulations for conducting communal acts. These regulations also bring to light the Buddha's concern to safeguard communal harmony. In order for a communal procedure to be valid for a Sangha living in a particular locality, all residents (whether permanent or visiting) must either be present or, if they cannot participate directly (for instance, because of illness), they must have given their consent for the procedure to take place in their absence. Transactions are divided into four categories: those that can be authorized merely on the basis of an announcement; those that require a motion; those that require a motion and a single proclamation; and those that require a motion and three proclamations. Those acts that require a more complex procedure are considered more important than those that can pass with a simpler procedure. Thus an act of ordination, by which a new candidate is admitted to the Sangha, is considered an important procedure that requires a motion and three proclamations, while appointing a monk as a distributor of meals requires only a motion and one proclamation. During the procedure, the members of the community give their consent by remaining silent. All present are invited to voice any objection during the process, and if there are no objections, the transaction is declared to have taken place.[3]

To maintain harmony in the monastic community, the Buddha laid down a set of guidelines known as the six principles of cordiality (*dhammā sāraṇīyā*), included here as **Text VII,3(3)**. These principles are extolled as "leading to affection, respect, concord, harmony, non-dispute, and unity." Originally intended for the monastic order, with suitable modifications they can be adopted by other intentional communities. Their emphasis on reciprocal kindness, good conduct, and sharing of gains makes them a strong antidote to the individualism and selfishness that can divide communities and tear them asunder. On an extended interpretation, where the text speaks of sharing the contents of the almsbowl, this can be understood to imply the sharing of resources and the social redistribution of revenues to eliminate flagrant disparities of wealth. Where the text speaks of harmony of views, in a pluralistic society this can be interpreted to mean mutual respect and tolerance among those holding diverse views. Ten additional principles of cordiality, similarly described but with a more monastic focus, are laid out in **Text VII,3(4).**

As was common in India during his time, the Buddha was occasionally approached by leaders of civil society and asked for advice about promoting cohesion within their own communities. In response he laid down seven principles designed to foster social harmony. The locus classicus for this is found in **Text VII,3(5)**, where he teaches "seven conditions for non-decline" to the Vajjis, a confederation of patrician republics centered around the thriving city of Vesālī. The seven conditions were intended to ensure that the Vajjis could withstand the challenges posed by neighboring monarchies, particularly the state of Magadha, whose king was keen on absorbing their territory into his realm. On occasion the Buddha took guidelines originally intended for civil society and then, with appropriate alterations, prescribed them to the monastic order. This is done with the seven principles for non-decline in **Text VII,3(6)**, a version that suits the situation of the monks.

The next text, **VII,3(7)**, deals with a specific aspect of communal living, care for the sick. Here the Buddha enumerates five desirable qualities of a nurse and five desirable qualities of a patient. Although he seems to be speaking of care for the sick in a monastery, where professional nursing care is generally not available, the same qualities can serve as guideposts for care for a patient in household life.

As is well known, Indian society during the Buddha's time was divided into four castes or social estates, determined on the basis of birth. There were the *khattiyas* (Sanskrit *kshatriyas*), the aristocratic or administrative caste; the *brāhmaṇas*, the priestly caste; the *vessas* (*vaishyas*), the merchants and agriculturists; and the suddas (*śūdras*), the menial workers and other laborers. Outside the fourfold class system were those without caste status, known as outcasts, people working in the very lowest occupations, such as trash collectors, latrine cleaners, and cremation ground attendants. In this chapter I present the Buddha's attitude to caste within the monastic order; in the last chapter I will deal with the Buddhist view of caste status in secular society. Within the monastic order, the Buddha regarded caste status as irrelevant. In **Text VII,4(1)** he says that, just as the waters of the great Indian rivers, on reaching the ocean, give up the names of their rivers and become known simply as "water of the ocean," so people from all four castes who join the Sangha give up their caste status and become known simply as followers of the Sakyan sage. In **Text VII,4(2)** he declares that people from any caste background who enter the homeless life can develop an exalted mind of loving-kindness and, going still further, can attain the final goal, the destruction of all defilements. **Text VII,4(3)**, addressed to King Pasenadi, states that anyone who abandons the five mental hindrances and attains the five perfections of an arahant is a supreme field of merit regardless of caste background.

Text VII,5 offers a shining account of a small group of monks who lived together in perfect unity, blending like milk and water. The secret to their success, they say, is that each puts aside what he wants and considers what the others want. In such a way, though they are different in body, they are one in mind.

In a Buddhist society harmony is essential not only within the lay community and the monastic order as they conduct their separate internal affairs, but also between the two communities in their mutual interactions. Thus the last section of this chapter is devoted to collaboration between the monastic and lay communities. **Text VII,6(1)** states categorically that the teaching flourishes when the two branches of the Buddhist community recognize their specific obligations toward one another and support each other in a spirit of shared appreciation. The following three suttas, **Texts VII,6(2)–(4)**, illustrate this from both points of view, showing the proper way for laypeople to treat monastics and for monastics to treat laypeople. It should be borne in mind that the standards of conduct set forth here presuppose the ancient Indian culture out of which Buddhism arose—a time when laypeople rarely had access to the higher teachings and were generally concerned with meritorious practices leading to a heavenly rebirth. In today's world, when laypeople can study the Dhamma in depth and undertake periods of intensive practice, changes in these specific relationships will naturally follow. However, if harmony is to prevail between the two communities, the spirit of respect and kindness that informs these relationships must remain a constant.

VII. The Intentional Community

1. KINDS OF COMMUNITIES

(1) The Shallow and the Deep

"Monks, there are these two kinds of communities. What two? The shallow community and the deep community.

"And what is the shallow community? The community in which the monks are restless, puffed up, vain, talkative, rambling in their talk, with muddled mindfulness, lacking in clear comprehension, unconcentrated, with wandering minds, with loose sense faculties: this is called the shallow community.

"And what is the deep community? The community in which the monks are not restless, puffed up, vain, talkative, and rambling in their talk, but have established mindfulness, clearly comprehend, are concentrated, with one-pointed minds and restrained sense faculties: this is called the deep community.

"These are the two kinds of communities. Of these two kinds of communities, the deep community is foremost."

(AN 2:42, NDB 161)

(2) The Divided and the Harmonious

"Monks, there are these two kinds of communities. What two? The divided community and the harmonious community.

"And what is the divided community? The community in which the monks take to arguing and quarreling and fall into disputes, stabbing each other with piercing words: this is called the divided community.

"And what is the harmonious community? The community in which the monks dwell in concord, harmoniously, without disputes, blending like milk and water, viewing each other with eyes of affection: this is called the harmonious community.

"These are the two kinds of communities. Of these two kinds of communities, the harmonious community is foremost."

(AN 2:43, NDB 161)

(3) The Inferior and the Superior

"Monks, there are these two kinds of communities. What two? The community of the inferior and the community of the superior.

"And what is the community of the inferior? Here, in this kind of community the elder monks are luxurious and lax, leaders in backsliding, discarding the duty of solitude; they do not arouse energy for the attainment of the as-yet-unattained, for the achievement of the as-yet-unachieved, for the realization of the as-yet-unrealized. Those in the next generation follow their example. They too become luxurious and lax, leaders in backsliding, discarding the duty of solitude; they too do not arouse energy for the attainment of the as-yet-unattained, for the achievement of the as-yet-unachieved, for the realization of the as-yet-unrealized. This is called the community of the inferior.

"And what is the community of the superior? Here, in this kind of community the elder monks are not luxurious and lax but discard backsliding and take the lead in solitude; they arouse energy for the attainment of the as-yet-unattained, for the achievement of the as-yet-unachieved, for the realization of the as-yet-unrealized. Those in the next generation follow their example. They too do not become luxurious and lax but discard backsliding and take the lead in solitude; they too arouse energy for the attainment of the as-yet-unattained, for the achievement of the as-yet-unachieved, for the realization of the as-yet-unrealized. This is called the community of the foremost.

"These are the two kinds of communities. Of these two kinds of communities, the community of the superior is foremost."

(AN 2:44, NDB 161–62)

(4) The Ignoble and the Noble

"Monks, there are these two kinds of communities. What two? The community of the noble and the community of the ignoble.

"And what is the community of the ignoble? The community in which the monks do not understand as it really is: 'This is suffering; this is the origin of suffering; this is the cessation of suffering; this is the way leading to the cessation of suffering': this is called the community of the ignoble.

"And what is the community of the noble? The community in which the monks understand as it really is: 'This is suffering; this is the origin of suffering; this is the cessation of suffering; this is the way leading to the cessation of suffering': this is called the community of the noble.

"These are the two kinds of communities. Of these two kinds of communities, the community of the noble is foremost."

(AN 2:45, NDB 162–63)

(5) The Unrighteous and the Righteous

"Monks, there are these two kinds of communities. What two? The unrighteous community and the righteous community.

"And what is the unrighteous community? Here, in this community disciplinary acts contrary to the Dhamma are enacted and disciplinary acts in accordance with the Dhamma are not enacted; disciplinary acts contrary to the discipline are enacted and disciplinary acts in accordance with the discipline are not enacted. Disciplinary acts contrary to the Dhamma are put forward and disciplinary acts in accordance with the Dhamma are not put forward; disciplinary acts contrary to the discipline are put forward and disciplinary acts in accordance with the discipline are not put forward. This is called the unrighteous community. It is because it is unrighteous that in this community disciplinary acts contrary to the Dhamma are enacted . . . and disciplinary acts in accordance with the discipline are not put forward.

"And what is the righteous community? Here, in this community disciplinary acts that accord with the Dhamma are enacted and disciplinary acts contrary to the Dhamma are not enacted; disciplinary acts that accord with the discipline are enacted and disciplinary acts contrary to the discipline are not enacted. Disciplinary acts that accord with the Dhamma are put forward and disciplinary acts contrary to the Dhamma are not put forward; disciplinary acts that accord with the discipline are put forward and disciplinary acts contrary to the discipline are not put forward. This is called the righteous community. It is because it is righteous that in this community disciplinary acts that accord with the Dhamma are enacted . . . and disciplinary acts contrary to the discipline are not put forward.

"These are the two kinds of communities. Of these two kinds of communities, the righteous community is foremost."

(AN 2:49, NDB 165–66)

2. The Formation of Community

(1) How Beings Come Together and Unite

"Monks, it is by way of elements that beings come together and unite: those of a low disposition come together and unite with those of a low disposition. In the past they did so, in the future they will do so, and now at present they do so too. Just as excrement comes together and unites with excrement, urine with urine, spittle with spittle, pus with pus, and blood with blood, so too, it is by way of elements that beings come together and unite: those of a low disposition come together and unite with those of a low disposition. In the past they did so, in the future they will do so, and now at present they do so too.

"Monks, it is by way of elements that beings come together and unite: those of a good disposition come together and unite with those of a good disposition. In the past they did so, in the future they will do so, and now at present they do so too. Just as milk comes together and unites with milk, oil with oil, ghee with ghee, honey with honey, and molasses with molasses, so too, monks, it is by way of elements that beings come together and unite: those of a good disposition come together and unite with those of a good disposition. In the past they did so, in the future they will do so, and now at present they do so too."

(SN 14:16, CDB 640)

(2) Like Attracts Like

"Monks, it is by way of elements that beings come together and unite. Those lacking faith come together and unite with those lacking faith, the shameless with the shameless, those unafraid of wrongdoing with those unafraid of wrongdoing, the unlearned with the unlearned, the lazy with the lazy, the muddle-minded with the muddle-minded, the unwise with the unwise. In the past it was so; in the future it will be so; and now too at present it is so.

"Monks, it is by way of elements that beings come together and unite. Those having faith come together and unite with those having faith, those having a sense of shame with those having a sense of shame, those afraid of wrongdoing with those afraid of wrongdoing, the learned with the learned, the energetic with the energetic, the mindful with the mindful, the wise with the wise. In the past it was so; in the future it will be so; and now too at present it is so.

"Those who destroy life come together and unite with those who destroy life; those who take what is not given . . . who engage in sexual misconduct . . . who speak falsehood . . . who indulge in wine, liquor, and intoxicants come together and unite with those who indulge in intoxicants.

"Those who abstain from the destruction of life come together and unite with those who abstain from the destruction of life; those who abstain from taking what is not given . . . from sexual misconduct . . . from false speech . . . from wine, liquor, and intoxicants come together and unite with those who abstain from intoxicants."

"Those of wrong view come together and unite with those of wrong view; those of wrong intention . . . wrong speech . . . wrong action . . . wrong livelihood . . . wrong effort . . . wrong mindfulness . . . wrong concentration come together and unite with those of wrong concentration.

"Those of right view come together and unite with those of right view; those of right intention . . . right speech . . . right action . . . right livelihood . . . right effort . . . right mindfulness . . . right concentration come together and unite with those of right concentration."

(SN 14:17, 14:25, 14:28; CDB 641, 644, 645)

(3) Four Means of Embracing Others

"Monks, there are these four means of embracing others. What four? Giving, endearing speech, beneficent conduct, and impartiality. These are the four means of embracing others."

> Giving, endearing speech,
> beneficent conduct, and impartiality
> under diverse worldly conditions,
> as is suitable to fit each case:
> these means of embracing others
> are like the linchpin of a rolling chariot.
>
> If there were no such means of embracing others,
> neither mother nor father
> would be able to obtain esteem
> and veneration from their son.
>
> But these means of embracing exist,
> and therefore the wise respect them;
> thus they attain to greatness
> and are highly praised.

(AN 4:32, NDB 419–20)

3. Sustaining Community

(1) The Standard of Authority

The brahmin Vassakāra, chief minister of Magadha, asked the Venerable Ānanda: "Is there, Master Ānanda, any single monk who was appointed by the Buddha thus: 'He will be your refuge when I am gone,' and whom you now have recourse to?"[4]

"There is no single monk who was appointed by the Blessed One thus: 'He will be your refuge when I am gone,' and whom we now have recourse to."

"But is there, Master Ānanda, any single monk who has been chosen by the Sangha and appointed by a number of elder monks thus: 'He will be our refuge after the Blessed One has gone,' and whom you now have recourse to?"

"There is no single monk who has been chosen by the Sangha and appointed by a number of elder monks thus: 'He will be our refuge after the Blessed One has gone,' and whom we now have recourse to."

"But if you have no refuge, Master Ānanda, what is the cause for your concord?"

"We are not without a refuge, brahmin. We have a refuge; we have the Dhamma as our refuge."

"You say, Master Ānanda, that you have the Dhamma as your refuge. How should this be understood?"

"Brahmin, the Blessed One prescribed the course of training for monks and has laid down the Pātimokkha. On the *uposatha* days[5] as many of us as live in dependence upon a single village district meet together in unison, and when we meet we ask one who knows the Pātimokkha to recite it. If a monk remembers an offense or a transgression while the Pātimokkha is being recited, we deal with him according to the Dhamma in the way we have been instructed. It is not the worthy ones who deal with us; it is the Dhamma that deals with us."

(MN 108, MLDB 892–95)

(2) The Reasons for the Training Rules

The Venerable Upāli approached the Blessed One, paid homage to him, sat down to one side, and said to him: "Bhante, on how many grounds has the Tathāgata prescribed the training rules for his disciples and recited the Pātimokkha?"

"It is, Upāli, on ten grounds that the Tathāgata has prescribed the training rules for his disciples and recited the Pātimokkha. What ten? (1) For the well-being of the Sangha; (2) for the ease of the Sangha; (3) for keeping recalcitrant persons in check; (4) so that well-behaved monks can dwell at ease; (5) for the restraint of influxes pertaining to this present life; (6) for the dispelling of influxes pertaining to future lives; (7) so that non-believers might gain faith; and (8) for increasing the faith of the believers; (9) for the continuation of the good Dhamma; and (10) for promoting discipline. It is on these ten grounds that the Tathāgata has prescribed the training rules for his disciples and recited the Pātimokkha."

(AN 20:31, NDB 1387)

(3) Six Principles of Cordiality

"Monks, there are these six principles of cordiality that create affection and respect and conduce to cohesiveness, non-dispute, concord, and unity. What six?

(1) "Here, a monk maintains bodily acts of loving-kindness toward his fellow monks both openly and privately. This is a principle of cordial-

ity that creates affection and respect and conduces to cohesiveness, non-dispute, concord, and unity.

(2) "Again, a monk maintains verbal acts of loving-kindness toward his fellow monks both openly and privately. This, too, is a principle of cordiality that creates affection and respect. . . .

(3) "Again, a monk maintains mental acts of loving-kindness toward his fellow monks both openly and privately. This, too, is a principle of cordiality that creates affection and respect. . . .

(4) "Again, a monk shares without reservation any righteous gains that have been righteously obtained, including even the contents of his alms-bowl, and uses such things in common with his virtuous fellow monks. This, too, is a principle of cordiality that creates affection and respect. . . .

(5) "Again, a monk dwells both openly and privately possessing in common with his fellow monks virtuous behavior that is unbroken, flawless, unblemished, unblotched, freeing, praised by the wise, ungrasped, leading to concentration. This, too, is a principle of cordiality that creates affection and respect. . . .

(6) "Again, a monk dwells both openly and privately possessing in common with his fellow monks a view that is noble and emancipating, which leads out, for one who acts upon it, to the complete destruction of suffering. This, too, is a principle of cordiality that creates affection and respect. . . .

"These, monks, are the six principles of cordiality that create affection and respect and conduce to cohesiveness, to non-dispute, to concord, and to unity."

(AN 6:12, NDB 866–67; see MN 48, MLDB 420–21)

(4) Ten Principles of Cordiality

On one occasion a number of monks assembled in the assembly hall and were sitting together when they took to arguing and quarreling and fell into a dispute, stabbing each other with piercing words. Then, in the evening, the Blessed One emerged from seclusion and went to the assembly hall, where he sat down on the prepared seat. The Blessed One then addressed the monks: "Monks, what discussion were you engaged in just now as you were sitting together here? What was the conversation that was underway?"

"Here, Bhante, after our meal, on returning from our alms round, we assembled in the assembly hall and were sitting together when we took to arguing and quarreling and fell into a dispute, stabbing each other with piercing words."

"Monks, it is not suitable for you clansmen who have gone forth out of faith from the household life into homelessness to take to arguing and quarreling and to fall into a dispute, stabbing each other with piercing words.

"There are, monks, these ten principles of cordiality that create affection and respect and conduce to cohesiveness, to non-dispute, to concord, and to unity. What ten?

(1) "Here, a monk is virtuous; he dwells restrained by the Pātimokkha, possessed of good conduct and resort, seeing danger in minute faults. Having undertaken the training rules, he trains in them. Since a monk is virtuous . . . this is a principle of cordiality that creates affection and respect and conduces to cohesiveness, to non-dispute, to concord, and to unity.

(2) "Again, a monk has learned much, remembers what he has learned, and accumulates what he has learned. Those teachings that are good in the beginning, good in the middle, and good in the end, with the right meaning and phrasing, which proclaim the perfectly complete and pure spiritual life—such teachings as these he has learned much of, retained in mind, recited verbally, investigated mentally, and penetrated well by view. Since a monk has learned much . . . this is a principle of cordiality that creates affection and respect and conduces to unity.

(3) "Again, a monk has good friends, good companions, good comrades. Since a monk has good friends . . . this is a principle of cordiality that creates affection and respect and conduces to unity.

(4) "Again, a monk is easy to correct and possesses qualities that make him easy to correct; he is patient and receives instruction respectfully. Since a monk is easy to correct . . . this is a principle of cordiality that creates affection and respect and conduces to unity.

(5) "Again, a monk is skillful and diligent in attending to the diverse chores that are to be done for his fellow monks; he possesses appropriate investigation there, and he is able to carry out and arrange everything properly. Since a monk is skillful and diligent . . . this is a principle of cordiality that creates affection and respect and conduces to unity.

(6) "Again, a monk loves the Dhamma and is pleasing in his assertions, filled with a lofty joy pertaining to the Dhamma and discipline. Since a monk loves the Dhamma . . . this is a principle of cordiality that creates affection and respect and conduces to unity.

(7) "Again, a monk has aroused energy for abandoning unwholesome qualities and acquiring wholesome qualities; he is strong, firm in exertion, not casting off the duty of cultivating wholesome qualities. Since a monk has aroused energy . . . this is a principle of cordiality that creates affection and respect and conduces to unity.

(8) "Again, a monk is content with any kind of robe, almsfood, lodging, and medicines and provisions for the sick. Since a monk is content with any kind of robe . . . this is a principle of cordiality that creates affection and respect and conduces to unity.

(9) "Again, a monk is mindful, possessing supreme mindfulness and alertness, one who remembers and recollects what was done and said long ago. Since a monk is mindful . . . this is a principle of cordiality that creates affection and respect and conduces to unity.

(10) "Again, a monk is wise; he possesses the wisdom that discerns arising and passing away, which is noble and penetrative and leads to the complete destruction of suffering. Since a monk is wise . . . this is a principle of cordiality that creates affection and respect and conduces to unity.

"These, monks, are the ten principles of cordiality that create affection and respect and conduce to cohesiveness, to non-dispute, to concord, and to unity."

(AN 10:50, NDB 1399–1401)

(5) Seven Conditions for Social Harmony

On one occasion the Blessed One was dwelling at Vesālī at the Sārandada Shrine. Then a number of Licchavis approached the Blessed One, paid homage to him, and sat down to one side. The Blessed One said this to them: "I will teach you, Licchavis, seven principles of non-decline. Listen and attend closely. I will speak."

"Yes, Bhante," those Licchavis replied. The Blessed One said this: "And what, Licchavis, are the seven principles of non-decline?

(1) "Licchavis, as long as the Vajjis assemble often and hold frequent assemblies, only growth is to be expected for them, not decline.

(2) "As long as the Vajjis assemble in harmony, adjourn in harmony, and conduct the affairs of the Vajjis in harmony, only growth is to be expected for them, not decline.

(3) "As long as the Vajjis do not decree anything that has not been decreed or abolish anything that has already been decreed but undertake and follow the ancient Vajji principles as they have been decreed, only growth is to be expected for them, not decline.

(4) "As long as the Vajjis honor, respect, esteem, and venerate the Vajji elders and think they should be heeded, only growth is to be expected for them, not decline.

(5) "As long as the Vajjis do not abduct women and girls from their families and force them to live with them, only growth is to be expected for them, not decline.

(6) "As long as the Vajjis honor, respect, esteem, and venerate their traditional shrines, both those within the city and those outside, and do not neglect the righteous oblations as given and done to them in the past, only growth is to be expected for them, not decline.

(7) "As long as the Vajjis provide righteous protection, shelter, and guard for arahants, so that those arahants who have not yet come may arrive,

and those arahants who have already come may dwell at ease there, only growth is to be expected for them, not decline.

"Licchavis, as long as these seven principles of non-decline continue among the Vajjis, and the Vajjis are seen established in them, only growth is to be expected for them, not decline."

(AN 7:21, NDB 1009–10)

(6) Seven Conditions for Monastic Harmony

The Blessed One said to the monks: "Monks, I will teach you seven principles of non-decline. Listen and attend closely. I will speak."

"Yes, Bhante," those monks replied. The Blessed One said this: "And what, monks, are the seven principles of non-decline?

(1) "As long as the monks assemble often and hold frequent assemblies, only growth is to be expected for them, not decline.

(2) "As long as the monks assemble in harmony, adjourn in harmony, and conduct the affairs of the Sangha in harmony, only growth is to be expected for them, not decline.

(3) "As long as the monks do not decree anything that has not been decreed or abolish anything that has already been decreed, but undertake and follow the training rules as they have been decreed, only growth is to be expected for them, not decline.

(4) "As long as the monks honor, respect, esteem, and venerate those monks who are elders, of long standing, long gone forth, fathers and guides of the Sangha, and think they should be heeded, only growth is to be expected for them, not decline.

(5) "As long as the monks do not come under the control of arisen craving that leads to renewed existence, only growth is to be expected for them, not decline.

(6) "As long as the monks are intent on forest lodgings, only growth is to be expected for them, not decline.

(7) "As long as the monks each individually establish mindfulness so that well-behaved fellow monks who have not yet come may arrive, and so well-behaved fellow monks who have already come may dwell at ease there, only growth is to be expected for them, not decline.

"Monks, as long as these seven principles of non-decline continue among the monks, and the monks are seen established in them, only growth is to be expected for them, not decline."

(AN 7:23, NDB 1013–14)

(7) Attending on the Sick

"Monks, possessing five qualities, an attendant is qualified to take care of a patient. What five? (1) He is able to prepare medicine. (2) He knows what is beneficial and harmful, so that he withholds what is harmful and offers what is beneficial. (3) He takes care of the patient with a mind of loving-kindness, not for the sake of material rewards. (4) He is not disgusted at having to remove feces, urine, vomit, or spittle. (5) He is able from time to time to instruct, encourage, inspire, and gladden the patient with a Dhamma talk. Possessing these five qualities, an attendant is qualified to take care of a patient.

"Possessing five other qualities, a patient is easy to take care of. What five? (1) He does what is beneficial. (2) He observes moderation in what is beneficial. (3) He takes his medicine. (4) He accurately discloses his symptoms to his kind-hearted attendant; he reports, as fits the case, that his condition is getting worse, or getting better, or remaining the same. (5) He can patiently endure arisen bodily feelings that are painful, racking, sharp, piercing, harrowing, disagreeable, sapping one's vitality. Possessing these five qualities, a patient is easy to take care of."

(AN 5:123–24 combined, NDB 741–42)

4. Caste Is Irrelevant

(1) Merging Like the Rivers in the Ocean

"Just as, when the great rivers—the Ganges, the Yamunā, the Aciravatī, the Sarabhū and the Mahī—reach the great ocean, they give up their former names and designations and are simply called the great ocean, so too, when members of the four castes—khattiyas, brahmins, vessas, and suddas[6]— go forth from the household life into homelessness in the Dhamma and discipline proclaimed by the Tathāgata, they give up their former names and clans and are simply called ascetics following the Sakyan son."

(from AN 8:19, NDB 1144; Ud 5.5)

(2) All Can Realize the Highest Goal

"Suppose there was a pond with clear, agreeable cool water, transparent, with smooth banks, delightful. If a man, scorched and exhausted by hot weather, weary, parched, and thirsty, came from the east or from the west or from the north or from the south or from where you will, having reached the pond he would quench his thirst and his hot-weather fever. So too, if anyone from a clan of khattiyas goes forth from the home life into homelessness, or from a clan of brahmins or a clan of vessas or a clan of suddas, and after encountering the Dhamma and discipline proclaimed by the Tathāgata, he develops loving-kindness, compassion, altruistic joy, and equanimity, and thereby gains internal peace, then because of that internal peace he practices the way proper to the ascetic, I say.

"Monks, if anyone from a clan of khattiyas goes forth from the home life into homelessness, or from a clan of brahmins or a clan of vessas or a clan of suddas, and by realizing it for himself with direct knowledge he here and now enters upon and abides in the liberation of mind, liberation by wisdom, that is influx-free through the destruction of the influxes, then he is an ascetic because of the destruction of the influxes."

(from MN 40, MLDB 374–75)

(3) The Criteria of Spiritual Worth

[The Buddha is questioning King Pasenadi:] "What do you think, great king? Suppose you were at war and a battle was about to take place. Then a khattiya youth would arrive, one who is untrained, unskilled, unpracticed, inexperienced, timid, petrified, frightened, quick to flee. Would you employ that man?" – "Surely not, Bhante."

"Then a brahmin youth would arrive . . . a vessa youth . . . a sudda youth . . . who is untrained . . . quick to flee. Would you employ that man, and would you have any use for such a man?" – "Surely not, venerable sir."

"What do you think, great king? Suppose you are at war and a battle is about to take place. Then a khattiya youth would arrive, one who is trained, skilled, practiced, experienced, brave, courageous, bold, ready to stand his place. Would you employ that man?" – "I would, Bhante."

"Then a brahmin youth would arrive . . . a vessa youth . . . a sudda youth . . . who is trained . . . ready to stand his place. Would you employ that man?" – "I would, Bhante."

"So too, great king, when a person has gone forth from the household life into homelessness, no matter from what clan, if he has abandoned five factors and possesses five factors, then what is given to him is of great fruit. What five factors have been abandoned? Sensual desire, ill will, dullness and drowsiness, restlessness and remorse, and doubt. What five factors does he possess? He possesses the aggregate of virtue of one beyond training, the aggregate of concentration of one beyond training, the aggregate of wisdom of one beyond training, the aggregate of liberation of one beyond training, the aggregate of the knowledge and vision of liberation of one beyond training. Thus what is given to one who has abandoned five factors and who possesses five factors is of great fruit.

> "As a king intent on waging war
> Would employ a youth skilled with the bow,
> One endowed with strength and vigor,
> But not the coward on account of his birth—
> So even though he be of low birth,
> One should honor the person of noble conduct,

The sagely man in whom are established
The virtues of patience and gentleness."

(from SN 3:24; CDB 190–91)

5. A MODEL OF MONASTIC HARMONY

On one occasion when the Venerables Anuruddha, Nandiya, and Kimbila were living in the Gosinga Sāla-tree Wood, the Blessed One went to visit them. When they heard he had arrived, all three went to meet the Blessed One. One took his bowl and outer robe, one prepared a seat, and one set out water for washing the feet. The Blessed One sat down on the seat made ready and washed his feet. Then those three venerable ones paid homage to the Blessed One and sat down at one side. When they were seated, the Blessed One said to them: "I hope you are all keeping well, Anuruddha. I hope you are all comfortable and not having any trouble getting almsfood."

"We are keeping well, Blessed One, we are comfortable, and we are not having any trouble getting almsfood."

"I hope, Anuruddha, that you are all living in concord, with mutual appreciation, without disputing, blending like milk and water, viewing each other with kindly eyes."

"Surely, Bhante, we are living in concord, with mutual appreciation, without disputing, blending like milk and water, viewing each other with kindly eyes."

"But, Anuruddha, how do you live thus?"

"Bhante, as to that, I think: 'It is a gain for me, it is a great gain for me, that I am living with such companions in the holy life.' I maintain bodily acts of loving-kindness toward those venerable ones both openly and privately; I maintain verbal acts of loving-kindness toward them both openly and privately; I maintain mental acts of loving-kindness toward them both openly and privately. I consider: 'Why should I not set aside what I wish to do and do what they wish to do?' Then I set aside what I wish to do and do what they wish to do. We are different in body, but one in mind. That is how, Bhante, we are living in concord, with mutual appreciation, without disputing, blending like milk and water, viewing each other with kindly eyes."

"Good, good! I hope that you all abide diligent, ardent, and resolute."

"Surely, Bhante, we abide diligent, ardent, and resolute."

"But, Anuruddha, how do you abide thus?"

"Bhante, as to that, whichever of us returns first from the village with almsfood prepares the seats, sets out the water for drinking and for washing, and puts the refuse bucket in its place. Whichever of us returns last eats any food left over, if he wishes; otherwise he throws it away where there is no greenery or drops it into water where there is no life. He puts away the seats and the water for drinking and for washing. He puts away the refuse bucket after washing it and he sweeps out the refectory. Whoever notices that the pots of water for drinking, washing, or the latrine are low or empty takes care of them. If they are too heavy for him, he calls someone else by a signal of the hand and they move it by joining hands, but because of this we do not break out into speech. But every five days we sit together all night discussing the Dhamma. That is how we abide diligent, ardent, and resolute."

(from MN 31, MLDB 301–2)

6. Monastics and Laity

(1) Mutual Support

"Monks, householders are very helpful to you. They provide you with the requisites of robes, almsfood, lodgings, and medicines in time of sickness. And you, monks, are very helpful to householders, as you teach them the Dhamma that is good in the beginning, the middle, and the end, with the right meaning and wording, and you proclaim the spiritual life in its fulfillment and complete purity. Thus, monks, this spiritual life is lived with mutual support for the purpose of crossing the flood and making a complete end of suffering."

(It §107)

(2) A Visitor of Families

"Monks, possessing five qualities, a monk who is a visitor of families is displeasing and disagreeable to them and is neither respected nor esteemed by them. What five? (1) He presumes intimacy upon mere acquaintance; (2) he distributes things that he does not own; (3) he consorts for the sake of creating divisions; (4) he whispers in the ear; and (5) he makes excessive requests. Possessing these five qualities, a monk who is a visitor of families is displeasing and disagreeable to them and is neither respected nor esteemed by them.

"Monks, possessing five other qualities, a monk who is a visitor of families is pleasing and agreeable to them and is respected and esteemed by them. What five? (1) He does not presume intimacy upon mere acquaintance; (2) he does not distribute things that he does not own; (3) he does not consort for the sake of creating divisions; (4) he does not whisper in the ear; and (5) he does not make excessive requests. Possessing these five qualities, a monk who is a visitor of families is pleasing and agreeable to them and is respected and esteemed by them."

(AN 5:111, NDB 736)

(3) Showing Compassion to Laypeople

"Monks, possessing five qualities, a resident monk shows compassion to laypeople. What five? (1) He encourages them in regard to virtuous behavior. (2) He settles them in understanding of the Dhamma. (3) When they are ill he approaches them and reminds them to establish mindfulness on the arahants. (4) When a large company of monks has arrived, including monks from various states, he approaches laypeople and informs them: 'Friends, a large company of monks has arrived including monks from various states. Make merit. It is an occasion to make merit.' (5) He himself eats whatever food they give him, whether coarse or excellent; he does not squander what has been given out of faith. Possessing these five qualities, a resident monk shows compassion to laypeople."

(AN 5:235, NDB 832)

(4) Families Worth Approaching

"Monks, possessing nine factors, a family that has not yet been approached is not worth approaching, or one that has been approached is not worth sitting with. What nine? (1) They do not rise up in an agreeable way. (2) They do not pay homage in an agreeable way. (3) They do not offer a seat in an agreeable way. (4) They hide what they have from one. (5) Even when they have much, they give little. (6) Even when they have excellent things, they give coarse things. (7) They give without respect, not respectfully. (8) They do not sit close by to listen to the Dhamma. (9) They do not savor the flavor of one's words. Possessing these nine factors, a family that has not yet been approached is not worth approaching, or one that has been approached is not worth sitting with.

"Monks, possessing nine factors, a family that has not yet been approached is worth approaching or one that has been approached is worth sitting with. What nine? (1) They rise up in an agreeable way. (2) They pay homage in an agreeable way. (3) They offer a seat in an agreeable way. (4) They do not hide what they have from one. (5) When they have much, they give much. (6) When they have excellent things, they give excellent things. (7) They give respectfully, not without respect. (8) They sit close by to listen to the Dhamma. (9) They savor the flavor of one's words. Possessing these nine factors, a family that has not yet been approached is worth approaching, or one that has been approached is worth sitting with."

(AN 9:17, NDB 1270–71)

VIII. Disputes

Introduction

Since communities, whether large or small, are composed of human beings, they are inevitably exposed to tensions caused by human frailties. The innate propensity for self-aggrandizement, craving for personal benefits, self-righteousness, and attachment to personal opinions can lead to factionalism and disputes and even split the community into fragments. Such disputes are the subject of Part VIII, and the settlement of disputes the subject of Part IX.

The passages included in Part VIII deal with disputes among both monastics and laity, which are similar in some respects but different in others. **Text VIII,1** sets up the theme of the chapter. We here see Sakka, ruler of the gods, come to the Buddha and present him with a conundrum: "When beings all wish to live in peace, why are they perpetually embroiled in conflict?" The Buddha's answer initiates a dialogue that pursues the origins of conflict down to increasingly subtler levels.

In **Text VIII,2** the elder monk Mahākaccāna states that laypeople quarrel with each other because of their attachment to sensual pleasures while ascetics quarrel with each other because of their attachment to views. **Texts VIII,3–6** illustrate his point: the first two texts in this group deal with disputes among householders and the last two with disputes among ascetics. While Mahākaccāna's thesis may have partial validity, the course of history actually shows the situation to be more complex. There have been wars between nations and regional blocs over rival ideologies—witness the Cold War that pitted corporate capitalism against communism, and the present-day hostilities between Sunni and Shiite Muslims. On the other hand, for the sake of their material requisites, grants of land, support from householders, as well as fame and honor, ascetics have engaged in bitter conflicts with one another and have even initiated lawsuits for material gain.

Since the Buddha placed the Sangha—the order of monks and nuns—at the core of the spiritual community, he recognized that the longevity of the Dhamma depended on the ability of his ordained disciples to contain disputes fomented in their ranks and re-establish unity. Conflict did indeed break out, the most famous being the quarrel that divided the monks of Kosambī along with their lay followers into two hostile factions whose mutual animosity was so strong that they even rejected the Buddha's efforts to intercede, as seen in **Text VIII,7**.[1]

To prevent disputes from breaking out in the monastic order, the Buddha devoted several discourses to their causes and the means of settling them once they have arisen. In **Text VIII,8**, he points out "six roots of disputes" (*vivādamūla*); since the first five occur in matching pairs, when they are counted separately the roots of dispute actually amount to eleven. Preventing disputes requires the monastics to remove the roots of dispute that might emerge in their midst before they deteriorate into full-scale divisions.

If conflicts become serious, they pose the further danger of schism, the division of the monastic order into two rival factions that refuse to acknowledge the validity of one another's acts. The Buddha considered a schism in the Sangha to be one of the gravest threats to the success of his mission. I therefore close this part with **Text VIII,9**, which strings together several short suttas on the conditions that lead to schism in the Sangha and the consequences respectively for those who foment schism and those who unite a divided Sangha.

VIII. Disputes

1. Why Do Beings Live in Hate?

Sakka, ruler of the devas, asked the Blessed One: "Beings wish to live without hate, hostility, or enmity; they wish to live in peace. Yet they live in hate, harming one another, hostile, and as enemies. By what fetters are they bound, sir, that they live in such a way?"

[The Blessed One said:] "Ruler of the devas, it is the bonds of envy and miserliness that bind beings so that, although they wish to live without hate, hostility, or enmity, and to live in peace, yet they live in hate, harming one another, hostile, and as enemies."

Sakka, delighted, exclaimed: "So it is, Blessed One, so it is, Fortunate One! Through the Blessed One's answer I have overcome my doubt and gotten rid of uncertainty." Then Sakka, having expressed his appreciation, asked another question: "But, sir, what gives rise to envy and miserliness, what is their origin, how are they born, how do they arise? When what is present do they arise, and when what is absent do they not arise?"

"Envy and miserliness arise from liking and disliking; this is their origin, this is how they are born, how they arise. When these are present, they arise, when these are absent, they do not arise."

"But, sir, what gives rise to liking and disliking . . . ?" – "They arise from desire . . . ." – "And what gives rise to desire . . . ?" – "It arises from thinking. When the mind thinks about something, desire arises; when the mind thinks of nothing, desire does not arise." – "But, sir, what gives rise to thinking . . . ?"

"Thinking, ruler of the devas, arises from elaborated perceptions and notions.[2] When elaborated perceptions and notions are present, thinking arises. When elaborated perceptions and notions are absent, thinking does not arise."

(from DN 21, LDB 328–29)

131

2. Disputes among Laypeople, Disputes among Ascetics

A brahmin approached the Venerable Mahākaccāna and asked him: "Why is it, Master Kaccāna, that khattiyas fight with khattiyas, brahmins with brahmins, and householders with householders?"

"It is, brahmin, because of adherence to lust for sensual pleasures, bondage to sensual pleasures, that khattiyas fight with khattiyas, brahmins with brahmins, and householders with householders."

"Why is it, Master Kaccāna, that ascetics fight with ascetics?"

"It is, brahmin, because of adherence to lust for views, bondage to views, that ascetics fight with ascetics."

"Is there then anyone in the world who has overcome this adherence to lust for sensual pleasures and this adherence to lust for views?"

"There is."

"And who is that?"

"In the town to the east called Sāvatthī, the Blessed One, the Arahant, the Perfectly Enlightened One is now dwelling. The Blessed One has overcome this adherence to lust for sensual pleasures and this adherence to lust for views."

When this was said, the brahmin rose from his seat, arranged his upper robe over one shoulder, lowered his right knee to the ground, reverently saluted in the direction of the Blessed One, and uttered this inspired utterance three times: "Homage to the Blessed One, the Arahant, the Perfectly Enlightened One! Homage to the Blessed One, the Arahant, the Perfectly Enlightened One! Homage to the Blessed One, the Arahant, the Perfectly Enlightened One! Indeed, that Blessed One has overcome this adherence to lust for sensual pleasures and this adherence to lust for views."

(AN 2:37, NDB 157–58)

3. Conflicts Due to Sensual Pleasures

"Again, with sensual pleasures as the cause, sensual pleasures as the source, sensual pleasures as the basis, the cause being simply sensual pleasures, kings quarrel with kings, nobles with nobles, brahmins with brahmins, householders with householders; mother quarrels with son, son with mother, father with son, son with father; brother quarrels with brother, brother with sister, sister with brother, friend with friend. And here in their quarrels, brawls, and disputes they attack each other with fists, clods, sticks, or knives, whereby they incur death or deadly suffering. Now this too is a danger in the case of sensual pleasures, a mass of suffering here and now, the cause being simply sensual pleasures.

"Again, with sensual pleasures as the cause men take swords and shields and buckle on bows and quivers, and they charge into battle massed in double array with arrows and spears flying and swords flashing; and there they are wounded by arrows and spears, and their heads are cut off by swords, whereby they incur death or deadly suffering. Now this too is a danger in the case of sensual pleasures, a mass of suffering here and now, the cause being simply sensual pleasures.

"Again, with sensual pleasures as the cause men take swords and shields and buckle on bows and quivers, and they charge slippery bastions, with arrows and spears flying and swords flashing; and there they are wounded by arrows and spears and splashed with boiling liquids and crushed under heavy weights, and their heads are cut off by swords, whereby they incur death or deadly suffering. Now this too is a danger in the case of sensual pleasures, a mass of suffering here and now, the cause being simply sensual pleasures."

(from MN 13, MLDB 181–82)

4. Rooted in Craving

"I will teach you, monks, nine things rooted in craving. Listen and attend closely. I will speak." – "Yes, Bhante," those monks replied. The Blessed One said this:

"And what are the nine things rooted in craving? (1) In dependence on craving there is seeking. (2) In dependence on seeking there is gain. (3) In dependence on gain there is judgment. (4) In dependence on judgment there is desire and lust. (5) In dependence on desire and lust there is attachment. (6) In dependence on attachment there is possessiveness. (7) In dependence on possessiveness there is miserliness. (8) In dependence on miserliness there is safeguarding. (9) With safeguarding as the foundation originate the taking up of rods and weapons, quarrels, contentions, and disputes, accusations, divisive speech, and false speech, and many other bad unwholesome things. These are the nine things rooted in craving."[3]

(AN 9:23, NDB 1280)

5. The Blind Men and the Elephant

On one occasion the Blessed One was living at Sāvatthī in Jeta's Grove, Anāthapiṇḍika's Park. Now at that time a number of ascetics and brahmins, wanderers of other sects, were living around Sāvatthī. They held various views, beliefs, and opinions, and propagated various views. And they were quarrelsome, disputatious, wrangling, wounding each other with verbal darts, saying, "The Dhamma is like this, the Dhamma is not like that! The Dhamma is not like this, the Dhamma is like that!"

Then a number of monks entered Sāvatthī on alms round. Having returned, after their meal they approached the Blessed One, paid homage to him, sat down to one side, and told him what they had seen. The Blessed One said: "Monks, wanderers of other sects are blind and sightless. They do not know what is beneficial and harmful. They do not know what is the Dhamma and what is not the Dhamma, and thus they are so quarrelsome and disputatious.

"Formerly, monks, there was a king in Sāvatthī who asked his servant to round up all the persons in the city who were blind from birth. When the man had done so, the king asked the servant to show the blind men an elephant. To some of the blind men he presented the elephant's head, to some the ear, to others a tusk, the trunk, the body, a foot, the hindquarters, the tail, or the tuft at the end of the tail. And to each one he said, 'This is an elephant.'

"When he reported to the king what he had done, the king went to the blind men and asked them: 'What is an elephant like?'

"Those who had been shown the head replied, 'An elephant, your majesty, is just like a water jar.' Those who had been shown the ear replied, 'An elephant is just like a winnowing basket.' Those who had been shown the tusk replied, 'An elephant is just like a plowshare.' Those who had been shown the trunk replied, 'An elephant is just like a plow pole.' Those who had been shown the body replied, 'An elephant is just like a storeroom.' And each of the others likewise described the elephant in terms of the part they had been shown.

"Then, saying, 'An elephant is like this, an elephant is not like that! An elephant is not like this, an elephant is like that!' they fought each other with their fists. And the king was delighted. Even so, monks, are the wanderers of other sects blind and sightless, and thus they become quarrelsome, disputatious, and wrangling, wounding each other with verbal darts."

(Ud 6.4)

6. Arguments among Monks

"Monks, wherever monks take to arguing and quarreling and fall into a dispute, stabbing each other with piercing words, I am uneasy even about directing my attention there, let alone about going there. I conclude about them: 'Surely, those venerable ones have abandoned three things and cultivated three other things.'

"What are the three things they have abandoned? Thoughts of renunciation, thoughts of benevolence, and thoughts of non-harming: these are the three things they have abandoned. What are the three things they have cultivated? Sensual thoughts, thoughts of ill will, and thoughts of harming: these are the three things they have cultivated. Wherever monks take to arguing and quarreling and fall into a dispute, I conclude: 'Surely, those venerable ones have abandoned these three things and cultivated these three other things.'

"Monks, wherever monks are dwelling in concord, harmoniously, without disputes, blending like milk and water, viewing each other with eyes of affection, I am at ease about going there, let alone about directing my attention there. I conclude: 'Surely, those venerable ones have abandoned three things and cultivated three other things.'

"What are the three things they have abandoned? Sensual thoughts, thoughts of ill will, and thoughts of harming: these are the three things they have abandoned. What are the three things they have cultivated? Thoughts of renunciation, thoughts of benevolence, and thoughts of nonharming. These are the three things they have cultivated. Wherever monks are dwelling in concord, I conclude: 'Surely, those venerable ones have abandoned these three things and cultivated these three other things.'"

(AN 3:124, NDB 354–55)

7. The Quarrel at Kosambī

Now on that occasion the monks at Kosambī had taken to arguing and quarreling and had fallen into a dispute, stabbing each other with piercing words. Then a certain monk went to the Blessed One, and after paying homage to him, he stood at one side and said: "Bhante, the monks here at Kosambī have taken to arguing and quarreling and have fallen into a dispute, stabbing each other with piercing words. It would be good, Bhante, if the Blessed One would go to those monks out of compassion." The Blessed One consented in silence.

Then the Blessed One went to those monks and said to them: "Enough, monks, let there be no arguing and quarreling and dispute." When this was said, a certain monk said to the Blessed One: "Wait, Bhante! Let the Blessed One, the Lord of the Dhamma, live at ease devoted to a pleasant abiding here and now. We are the ones who will be responsible for this dispute."

For a second time . . . For a third time the Blessed One said: "Enough, monks, let there be no no arguing and quarreling and dispute." For a third time that monk said to the Blessed One: "Wait, Bhante! . . . We are the ones who will be responsible for this dispute."

Then, when it was morning, the Blessed One dressed, and taking his bowl and outer robe, entered Kosambī for alms. When he had wandered for alms in Kosambī and had returned from his alms round, after his meal he set his resting place in order, took his bowl and outer robe, and while still standing uttered these stanzas:

"When many voices shout at once
none considers himself a fool;
though the Sangha is being split
none thinks himself to be at fault.

"They have forgotten thoughtful speech,
talking obsessed by words alone.
Uncurbed their mouths, they bawl at will;
none knows what leads him so to act.

"'He abused me, he struck me,
he defeated me, he robbed me'—
in those who harbor thoughts like these
enmity will never be allayed.

"For in this world enmity is never
allayed by enmity.
It is allayed by non-hatred:
that is the fixed and ageless law.

"Those others do not recognize
that here we should restrain ourselves.
But those wise ones who realize this
at once end all their enmity.

"Breakers of bones and murderers,
those who steal cattle, horses, wealth,
those who pillage the entire realm—
when even these can act together
why can you not do so too?

"If one can find a worthy friend,
a virtuous, steadfast companion,
then overcome all threats of danger
and walk with him content and mindful.

"But if one finds no worthy friend,
no virtuous, steadfast companion,
then as a king leaves his conquered realm,
walk like a tusker in the woods alone.

"Better it is to walk alone;
there is no companionship with fools.

> Walk alone and do no evil,
>   at ease like a tusker in the woods."

(from MN 128, MLDB 1008–10)

8. Roots of Disputes

"Monks, there are these six roots of disputes. What six?

(1) "Here, a monk is angry and hostile. When a monk is angry and hostile, he dwells without respect and deference toward the Teacher, the Dhamma, and the Sangha, and he does not fulfill the training. Such a monk creates a dispute in the Sangha that leads to the harm of many people, to the unhappiness of many people, to the ruin, harm, and suffering of devas and humans. If, monks, you perceive any such root of dispute either in yourselves or in others, you should strive to abandon this evil root of dispute. And if you do not perceive any such root of dispute either in yourselves or in others, you should practice so that this evil root of dispute does not emerge in the future. In such a way this evil root of dispute is abandoned and does not emerge in the future.

(2) "Again, a monk is a denigrator and insolent . . . (3) . . . envious and miserly . . . (4) . . . crafty and hypocritical . . . (5) . . . one who has evil desires and wrong view . . . (6) . . . one who adheres to his own views, holds to them tenaciously, and relinquishes them with difficulty. Such a monk dwells without respect and deference toward the Teacher, the Dhamma, and the Sangha, and he does not fulfill the training. He creates a dispute in the Sangha that leads to the harm of many people, to the unhappiness of many people, to the ruin, harm, and suffering of devas and humans. If, monks, you perceive any such root of dispute either in yourselves or in others, you should strive to abandon this evil root of dispute. And if you do not perceive any such root of dispute either in yourselves or others, you should practice so that this evil root of dispute does not emerge in the future. In such a way this evil root of dispute is abandoned and does not emerge in the future.

"These, monks, are the six roots of dispute."

(AN 6:36, NDB 898–99; MN 104, MLDB 854–55)

9. Schism in the Sangha

The Venerable Upāli approached the Blessed One, paid homage to him, sat down to one side, and said to him: "Bhante, it is said: 'Schism in the Sangha, schism in the Sangha.' How, Bhante, is there schism in the Sangha?"

"Here, Upāli, (1) monks explain non-Dhamma as Dhamma, (2) and Dhamma as non-Dhamma. (3) They explain non-discipline as discipline, and (4) discipline as non-discipline. (5) They explain what has not been stated and uttered by the Tathāgata as having been stated and uttered by him, and (6) what has been stated and uttered by the Tathāgata as not having been stated and uttered by him. (7) They explain what has not been practiced by the Tathāgata as having been practiced by him, and (8) what has been practiced by the Tathāgata as not having been practiced by him. (9) They explain what has not been prescribed by the Tathāgata as having been prescribed by him, and (10) what has been prescribed by the Tathāgata as not having been prescribed by him. On these ten grounds they withdraw and go apart. They perform legal acts separately and recite the Pātimokkha separately. It is in this way, Upāli, that there is schism in the Sangha."

"Bhante, it is said: 'Concord in the Sangha, concord in the Sangha.' How is there concord in the Sangha?"

"Here, Upāli, (1) monks explain non-Dhamma as non-Dhamma, and (2) Dhamma as Dhamma. (3) They explain non-discipline as non-discipline, and (4) discipline as discipline. (5) They explain what has not been stated and uttered by the Tathāgata as not having been stated and uttered by him, and (6) what has been stated and uttered by the Tathāgata as having been stated and uttered by him. (7) They explain what has not been practiced by the Tathāgata as not having been practiced by him, and (8) what has been practiced by the Tathāgata as having been practiced by him. (9) They explain what has not been prescribed by the Tathāgata as not having been prescribed by him, and (10) what has been prescribed by the Tathāgata as having been prescribed by him. On these ten grounds, they do not withdraw and go apart. They do not perform legal acts separately or recite the Pātimokkha separately. It is in this way, Upāli, that there is concord in the Sangha."

On another occasion the Venerable Ānanda approached the Blessed One, paid homage to him, sat down to one side, and said to him: "Bhante, when one causes schism in a harmonious Sangha, what does one generate?" – "One generates evil lasting for an eon." – "But, Bhante, what is that evil lasting for an eon?" – "One is tormented in hell for an eon."

> One who causes schism in the Sangha is bound for misery,
> bound for hell, to abide there for an eon.
> Delighting in factions, established in non-Dhamma,
> he falls away from security from bondage.
> Having caused schism in a harmonious Sangha,
> he is tormented in hell for an eon.

Then the Venerable Ānanda asked: "Bhante, when one reconciles a divided Sangha, what does one generate?" – "One generates divine merit,

Ānanda." – "But, Bhante, what is divine merit?" – "One rejoices in heaven for an eon, Ānanda."

> Pleasant is concord in the Sangha,
> and the mutual help of those who live in concord.
> Delighting in concord, established in Dhamma,
> one does not fall away from security from bondage.
> Having brought concord to the Sangha,
> one rejoices in heaven for an eon.

(AN 10:37–40 combined, NDB 1389–91)

IX. SETTLING DISPUTES

Introduction

Where the previous chapter was devoted to the origins of disputes, Part IX is devoted to the resolution of disputes. The easiest type of dispute to resolve is that between two people of good intentions. In monastic life such disputes often revolve around the rules of discipline. Thus **Text IX,1** shows that such a dispute can be nipped in the bud when the party at fault acknowledges his transgression as such, and the accuser accepts his apology and pardons him.

Following this comes a pair of suttas that were apparently spoken by the Buddha in his old age, perhaps toward the very end of his life. In **Text IX,2**, he lays down guidelines for settling differences of opinion over the interpretation of the Dhamma. It is significant that he here emphasizes the meaning of the doctrine above the letter, which he calls "trifling." In the same discourse he also offers advice about dealing with a transgressor. He insists that, even though the reproachful monk may find it troublesome to correct the offender, and though the offender may be hurt by the criticism, as long as one has any chance of changing the offender's conduct and helping him "emerge from the unwholesome and be established in the wholesome," one should speak to him. But, the Buddha says, when there is no chance of changing the offender's ways, and attempting to correct him might just make the situation worse, "one should not underrate equanimity toward such a person."

Text IX,3, according to its preamble, originated shortly after the death of Mahāvīra, the leader of the Jain community, known in the Pāli Canon as Nātaputta. After his death his followers split into two camps that bitterly attacked each other. The discourse here was spoken by the Buddha to prevent a similar fate from befalling his own community. The Buddha defines the primary threat to the success of his teaching to be disagreements over the thirty-seven aids to enlightenment. Disagreements about livelihood and the rules of training, he says, are of secondary importance. In this same discourse he explains how to settle disputes about the Dhamma and the Vinaya. The first two methods are to settle the disagreement among the disputants and to bring the disagreement to a larger community and abide by the decision of the majority. The last method, to be used when the others fail, is a procedure called "covering over with grass." This permits a representative monk on each side of the conflict to confess transgressions on behalf of the entire group—with exception made for major violations—without dwelling on the details. This method, which lets the past be past, circumvents the need to review the entire background to the conflict, which might only rekindle old resentments.

Text IX,4(1) stresses that to prevent disciplinary problems from flaring up and generating divisions, the monks involved—both the one who committed the transgression and the one who reproves him—should reflect on themselves, quell their antagonism toward each other, and achieve reconciliation. **Text IX,4(2)** insists that disciplinary issues should first be "settled internally," within one's own circle of followers, so that the dissension does not spread outward and embroil others.

The Buddha often insisted that for the Sangha to flourish, the monks and nuns must repeatedly correct, admonish, and encourage one another. The ideal attitude, according to **Text IX,5**, is threefold: to be open to receiving correction from others; to be willing to correct offenders, even one's elders, when the need arises; and to be ready to make amends for one's offenses. Receiving criticism from others, however, can sting the ego, provoking resistance and resentment. To address this problem, in the Discourse on Inference—included here as **Text IX,6**—the Venerable Moggallāna enumerates the qualities that make a monk resistant to correction and drives home the need for self-examination in order to remove those qualities.

Conflicts occasionally broke out between members of the lay community and the monastic order. In some instances the Buddha recognized that the behavior of a layperson called for an expression of disapproval from the Sangha; he thus allowed the monks to "overturn the almsbowl," that is, to refuse to accept offerings from an offensive lay follower.[1] The conditions under which such an action are permitted are stated in **Text IX,7(1)**. It was also recognized that lay followers might have justified complaints against a monk who was not living up to the standards of discipline expected of him. In response, laypeople are allowed to officially proclaim a "loss of confidence" in that monk, the conditions for which are explained in **Text IX,7(2)**. To facilitate reconciliation between the monk and the lay disciple, the Sangha could decide that a wayward monk must approach the layperson he had offended and apologize for his misbehavior, as shown in **Text IX,7(3)**.

Four rules for monks laid down in the Pātimokkha are called Pārājika, "expulsion offenses." These are sexual intercourse; theft (of an item above a certain threshold value); the taking of human life; and putting forth false claims to attainment of a "superhuman state," a psychic power or state of higher realization. A monk who transgresses these is no longer in communion with the monks and must be expelled from the Sangha.[2] Usually, monks or nuns who fall into these offenses will confess their transgression and voluntarily leave the monastic order. But there are cases when the offender conceals the transgression and tries to pass off as a legitimate member of the order. In such cases the Buddha does not hesitate to instruct the monks to expel the miscreant.

Texts IX,8(1)–(2) deal with just such a situation. In the first, the Buddha lays down the general principle that the wrongdoer who is posing as a regular monk must be expelled. He is just like chaff amid the barley. The second describes an incident when the Buddha refused to recite the Pātimokkha because a miscreant, "inwardly rotten, corrupt, depraved," was sitting in the midst of the assembly. Moggallāna, discovering the evil-doer with his psychic powers, forcefully expelled him from the hall and bolted the door behind him.

IX. Settling Disputes

1. CONFESSION AND FORGIVENESS

Once two monks had a quarrel and one monk had transgressed against the other. Then the former monk confessed his transgression to the other monk, but the latter would not pardon him. Then a number of monks approached the Blessed One and reported what had happened. [The Blessed One said:] "Monks, there are two kinds of fools: one who does not see a transgression as a transgression; and one who, when another is confessing a transgression, does not pardon him. These are the two kinds of fools. There are two kinds of wise people: one who sees a transgression as a transgression; and one who, when another is confessing a transgression, pardons him. These are the two kinds of wise people."

(SN 11:24, CDB 339)

2. RESOLVING DIFFERENCES IN OPINION

"While you are training in concord, with mutual appreciation, without disputing, two monks might make different assertions concerning the Dhamma.[3]

"Now if you should think thus: 'These venerable ones differ about both the meaning and the phrasing,' then whichever monk you think is the more reasonable should be approached and addressed thus: 'The venerable ones differ about both the meaning and the phrasing. The venerable ones should know that it is for this reason that there is difference about the meaning and difference about the phrasing; let them not fall into a dispute.' Then whichever monk you think is the most reasonable of those who side together on the opposite part should be approached and addressed thus: 'The venerable ones differ about the meaning and the phrasing. The venerable ones should know that it is for this reason that there is difference about the meaning and difference about the phrasing; let them not fall into a dispute.' So what has been wrongly grasped should be borne in mind as wrongly grasped. Bearing in mind what has been wrongly grasped as wrongly grasped, what is Dhamma and what is discipline should be expounded.

"Now if you should think thus: 'These venerable ones differ about the meaning but agree about the phrasing,' then whichever monk you think is the more reasonable should be approached and addressed thus: 'The venerable ones differ about the meaning but agree about the phrasing. The venerable ones should know that it is for this reason that there is difference about the meaning but agreement about the phrasing; let them not fall into a dispute.' Then whichever monk you think is the most reasonable of those who side together on the opposite part should be approached and addressed thus: 'The venerable ones differ about the meaning but agree about the phrasing. The venerable ones should know that it is for this reason that there is difference about the meaning but agreement about the phrasing; let them not fall into a dispute.' So what has been wrongly grasped should be borne in mind as wrongly grasped and what has been rightly grasped should be borne in mind as rightly grasped. Bearing in mind what has been wrongly grasped as wrongly grasped, and bearing in mind what has been rightly grasped as rightly grasped, what is Dhamma and what is discipline should be expounded.

"Now if you think thus: 'These venerable ones agree about the meaning but differ about the phrasing,' then whichever monk you think is the more reasonable should be approached and addressed thus: 'The venerable ones agree about the meaning but differ about the phrasing. The venerable ones should know that it is for this reason that there is agreement about the meaning but difference about the phrasing. But the phrasing is a mere trifle. Let the venerable ones not fall into a dispute over a mere trifle.' Then whichever monk you think is the most reasonable of those who side together on the opposite part should be approached and addressed thus: 'The venerable ones agree about the meaning but differ about the phrasing. The venerable ones should know that it is for this reason that there is agreement about the meaning but difference about the phrasing. But the phrasing is a mere trifle. Let the venerable ones not fall into a dispute over a mere trifle.' So what has been rightly grasped should be borne in mind as rightly grasped and what has been wrongly grasped should be borne in mind as wrongly grasped. Bearing in mind what has been rightly grasped as rightly grasped, and bearing in mind what has been wrongly grasped as wrongly grasped, what is Dhamma and what is discipline should be expounded.

"Now if you should think thus: 'These venerable ones agree about both the meaning and the phrasing,' then whichever monk you think is the more reasonable should be approached and addressed thus: 'The venerable ones agree about both the meaning and the phrasing. The venerable ones should know that it is for this reason that there is agreement about both the meaning and the phrasing; let the venerable ones not fall into a dispute.' Then whichever monk you think is the most reasonable of those who side together on the opposite part should be approached and addressed thus: 'The venerable ones agree about both the meaning and the phrasing. The venerable ones should know that it is for this reason that there is agreement about both the meaning and the phrasing; let the venerable ones not fall into a dispute.' So what has been rightly grasped should be borne in mind as rightly grasped. Bearing in mind what has been rightly grasped as rightly grasped, what is Dhamma and what is discipline should be expounded.

"While you are training in concord, with mutual appreciation, without disputing, some monk might commit an offense or a transgression. Now, monks, you should not hurry to reprove him; rather, the person should be examined thus: 'I shall not be troubled and the other person will not be hurt; for the other person is not given to anger and resentment, he is not firmly attached to his view and he relinquishes easily, and I can make that person emerge from the unwholesome and establish him in the wholesome.' If such occurs to you, monks, it is proper to speak.

"Then it may occur to you, monks: 'I shall not be troubled, but the other person will be hurt, for the other person is given to anger and resentment. However, he is not firmly attached to his view and he relinquishes easily, and I can make that person emerge from the unwholesome and establish him in the wholesome. It is a mere trifle that the other person will be hurt, but it is a much greater thing that I can make that person emerge from the unwholesome and establish him in the wholesome.' If such occurs to you, monks, it is proper to speak.

"Then it may occur to you, monks: 'I shall be troubled, but the other person will not be hurt; for the other person is not given to anger and resentment, though he is firmly attached to his view and he relinquishes with difficulty; yet I can make that person emerge from the unwholesome and establish him in the wholesome. It is a mere trifle that I shall be troubled, but it is a much greater thing that I can make that person emerge from the unwholesome and establish him in the wholesome.' If such occurs to you, monks, it is proper to speak.

"Then it may occur to you, monks: 'I shall be troubled and the other person will be hurt; for the other person is given to anger and resentment, and he is firmly attached to his view and he relinquishes with difficulty; yet I can make that person emerge from the unwholesome and establish him in the wholesome. It is a mere trifle that I shall be troubled and the other person hurt, but it is a much greater thing that I can make that person emerge from the unwholesome and establish him in the wholesome.' If such occurs to you, monks, it is proper to speak.

"Then it may occur to you, monks: 'I shall be troubled and the other person will be hurt; for the other person is given to anger and resentment, and he is firmly attached to his view and he relinquishes with difficulty;

and I cannot make that person emerge from the unwholesome and establish him in the wholesome.' One should not underrate equanimity toward such a person.

"While you are training in concord, with mutual appreciation, without disputing, there might arise mutual verbal friction, insolence in views, mental annoyance, bitterness, and dejection. Then whichever monk you think is the most reasonable of those who side together on the one part should be approached and addressed thus: 'While we were training in concord, friend, with mutual appreciation, without disputing, there arose mutual verbal friction, insolence in views, mental annoyance, bitterness, and dejection. If the Master knew, would he censure that?' Answering rightly, the monk would answer thus: 'If the Master knew, he would censure that.'

"'But, friend, without abandoning that thing, can one realize nibbāna?' Answering rightly, the monk would answer thus: 'Friend, without abandoning that thing, one cannot realize nibbāna.'

"Then whichever monk you think is the most reasonable of those who side together on the opposite part should be approached and addressed thus: 'While we were training in concord, friend, with mutual appreciation, without disputing, there arose mutual verbal friction, insolence in views, mental annoyance, bitterness, and dejection. If the Master knew, would he censure that?' Answering rightly, the monk would answer thus: 'If the Master knew, he would censure that.'

"'But, friend, without abandoning that thing, can one realize nibbāna?' Answering rightly, the monk would answer thus: 'Friend, without abandoning that thing, one cannot realize nibbāna.'

"If others should ask that monk thus: 'Was it the venerable one who made those monks emerge from the unwholesome and established them in the wholesome?' answering rightly, the monk would say: 'Here, friends, I went to the Blessed One. The Blessed One taught me the Dhamma. Having heard that Dhamma, I spoke to those monks. The monks heard that Dhamma, and they emerged from the unwholesome and became established in the wholesome.' Answering thus, the monk neither exalts himself nor disparages others; he answers in accordance with the Dhamma in such a way that nothing which provides a ground for censure can be legitimately deduced from his assertion."

That is what the Blessed One said. The monks were satisfied and delighted in the Blessed One's words.

(from MN 103, MLDB 848–52)

3. Settling Disputes in the Sangha

The Venerable Ānanda and the novice Cunda went together to the Blessed One. After paying homage to him, they sat down to one side, and the

Venerable Ānanda said to the Blessed One: "This novice Cunda, Bhante, says that the Jain teacher Nātaputta has just died.[4] On his death the Jains are divided, split into two, left without a refuge. I thought: 'Let no dispute arise in the Sangha when the Blessed One has gone. For such a dispute would be for the harm and unhappiness of many, for the loss, harm, and suffering of gods and humans.'"

"What do you think, Ānanda? These things that I have taught you after directly knowing them—that is, the four establishments of mindfulness, the four right kinds of striving, the four bases for spiritual power, the five faculties, the five powers, the seven enlightenment factors, the noble eightfold path—do you see, Ānanda, even two monks who make differing assertions about these things?"

"No, Bhante, I do not see even two monks who make differing assertions about these things. But, Bhante, there are people who live deferential toward the Blessed One who might, when he has gone, create a dispute in the Sangha about livelihood and about the Pātimokkha. Such a dispute would be for the harm and unhappiness of many, for the loss, harm, and suffering of gods and humans."

"A dispute about livelihood or about the Pātimokkha would be trifling, Ānanda. But should a dispute arise in the Sangha about the path or the way, such a dispute would be for the harm and unhappiness of many, for the loss, harm, and suffering of gods and humans.

"There are, Ānanda, these six roots of disputes. What six? Here, Ānanda, a monk is angry and hostile . . . [as in Text VIII,8] . . . one adheres to his own views, holds to them tenaciously, and relinquishes them with difficulty. Such a monk dwells without respect and deference toward the Teacher, the Dhamma, and the Sangha, and he does not fulfill the training. He creates a dispute in the Sangha that leads to the harm of many people, to the unhappiness of many people, to the ruin, harm, and suffering of devas and humans. If, monks, you perceive any such root of dispute either in yourselves or in others, you should strive to abandon this evil root of dispute. And if you do not perceive any such root of dispute either in yourselves or others, you should practice so that this evil root of dispute does not emerge in the future. In such a way this evil root of dispute is abandoned and does not emerge in the future. . . .

"And how is there removal [of a disciplinary issue] by presence? Here monks are disputing: 'It is Dhamma,' or 'It is not Dhamma,' or 'It is discipline,' or 'It is not discipline.' Those monks should all meet together in concord. Then, having met together, the guideline of the Dhamma should be drawn out. Once the guideline of the Dhamma has been drawn out, that disciplinary issue should be settled in a way that accords with it. Such is the removal of a disciplinary issue by presence. And so there comes to be the settlement of some disciplinary issues here in this way, through removal by presence.[5]

"And how is there the opinion of a majority? If those monks cannot settle that disciplinary issue in that dwelling place, they should go to a dwelling place where there is a greater number of monks. There they should all meet together in concord. Then, having met together, the guideline of the Dhamma should be drawn out.[6] Once the guideline of the Dhamma has been drawn out, that disciplinary issue should be settled in a way that accords with it. Such is the opinion of a majority. And so there comes to be the settlement of some disciplinary issues here by the opinion of a majority. . . .

"And how is there covering over with grass? Here when monks have taken to quarreling and brawling and are deep in disputes, they may have said and done many things improper for an ascetic. Those monks should all meet together in concord. When they have met together, a wise monk among the monks who side together on the one side should rise from his seat, and after arranging his robe on one shoulder, he should raise his hands, palms together, and call for an enactment of the Sangha thus: 'Let the venerable Sangha hear me. When we took to quarreling and brawling and were deep in disputes, we said and did many things improper for an ascetic. If it is approved by the Sangha, then for the good of these venerable ones and for my own good, in the midst of the Sangha I shall confess, by the method called 'covering over with grass,' any offenses of these venerable ones and any offenses of my own, except for those which call for serious censure and those connected with the laity.'

"Then a wise monk among the monks who side together on the other part should rise from his seat, and after arranging his robe on one shoulder, he should raise his hands, palms together, and call for an enactment of the Sangha thus: 'Let the venerable Sangha hear me. When we took to quarreling and brawling and were deep in disputes, we said and did many things improper for an ascetic. If it is approved by the Sangha, then for the good of these venerable ones and for my own good, in the midst of the Sangha I shall confess, by the method called 'covering over with grass,' any offenses of these venerable ones and any offenses of my own, except for those which call for serious censure and those connected with the laity.' Such is the covering over with grass. And so there comes to be the settlement of some disciplinary issues here by the covering over with grass."

(MN 104, MLDB 855–59)

4. DISPUTES OVER DISCIPLINE

(1) The Need for Self-Reflection

"Monks, if, in regard to a particular disciplinary issue, the monk who has committed an offense and the monk who reproves him do not thoroughly reflect upon themselves, it can be expected that this disciplinary issue will lead to acrimony and animosity for a long time and the monks will not dwell at ease. But if the monk who has committed an offense and the monk who reproves him thoroughly reflect upon themselves, it can be expected that this disciplinary issue will not lead to acrimony and animosity for a long time and the monks will dwell at ease.

"And how does the monk who has committed an offense thoroughly reflect upon himself? Here, the monk who has committed an offense reflects thus: 'I have committed a particular unwholesome misdeed with the body. That monk saw me doing so. If I had not committed a particular unwholesome misdeed with the body, he would not have seen me doing so. But because I committed a particular unwholesome misdeed with the body, he saw me doing so. When he saw me committing a particular unwholesome misdeed with the body, he became displeased. Being displeased, he expressed his displeasure to me. Because he expressed his displeasure to me, I became displeased. Being displeased, I informed others. Thus in this case I was the one who incurred a transgression, just as a traveler does when he evades the customs duty on his goods.' It is in this way that the monk who has committed an offense thoroughly reflects upon himself.

"And how does the reproving monk thoroughly reflect upon himself? Here, the reproving monk reflects thus: 'This monk has committed a particular unwholesome misdeed with the body. I saw him doing so. If this monk had not committed a particular unwholesome misdeed with the body, I would not have seen him doing so. But because he committed a particular unwholesome misdeed with the body, I saw him doing so. When I saw him committing a particular unwholesome misdeed with the body, I became displeased. Being displeased, I expressed my displeasure to him. Because I expressed my displeasure to him, he became displeased. Being displeased, he informed others. Thus in this case I was the one who incurred a transgression, just as a traveler does when he evades the customs duty on his goods.' It is in this way that the reproving monk thoroughly reflects upon himself.

"If, monks, in regard to a particular disciplinary issue, the monk who has committed an offense and the monk who reproves him do not each thoroughly reflect upon themselves, it can be expected that this disciplinary issue will lead to acrimony and animosity for a long time and the monks will not dwell at ease. But if the monk who has committed an offense and the monk who reproves him each thoroughly reflect upon themselves, it can be expected that this disciplinary issue will not lead to acrimony and animosity for a long time and the monks will dwell at ease."

(AN 2:15, NDB 145–47)

(2) Avoiding Acrimony

"Monks, when, in regard to a disciplinary issue, the exchange of words between both parties, the insolence about views, and the resentment, bitterness, and exasperation are not settled internally,[7] it can be expected that this disciplinary issue will lead to acrimony and animosity for a long time, and the monks will not dwell at ease.

"Monks, when, in regard to a disciplinary issue, the exchange of words between both parties, the insolence about views, and the resentment, bitterness, and exasperation are well settled internally, it can be expected that this disciplinary issue will not lead to acrimony and animosity for a long time, and the monks will dwell at ease."

(AN 2:63, NDB 170)

5. MUTUAL CORRECTION

"Monks, I will teach you about co-residency among the bad and about co-residency among the good. Listen and attend closely. I will speak."

"Yes, Bhante," those monks replied. The Blessed One said this:

"And how is there co-residency among the bad, and how do the bad live together? Here, it occurs to an elder monk: 'An elder—or one of middle standing or a junior—should not correct me. I should not correct an elder, or one of middle standing or a junior. If an elder corrects me, he might do so without sympathy, not sympathetically. I would then say "No!" to him and would trouble him, and even seeing [my offense] I would not make amends for it. If one of middle standing corrects me . . . If a junior corrects me, he might do so without sympathy, not sympathetically. I would then say "No!" to him and would trouble him, and even seeing [my offense] I would not make amends for it.'

"It occurs, too, to one of middle standing . . . to a junior: 'An elder—or one of middle standing or a junior—should not correct me. I should not correct an elder . . . and even seeing [my offense] I would not make amends for it.' It is in this way that there is co-residency among the bad, and it is in this way that the bad live together.

"And how, monks, is there co-residency among the good, and how do the good live together? Here, it occurs to an elder monk: 'An elder—and one of middle standing and a junior—should correct me. I should correct an elder, one of middle standing, and a junior. If an elder corrects me, he might do so sympathetically, not without sympathy. I would then say "Good!" to him and would not trouble him, and seeing [my offense] I would make amends for it. If one of middle standing corrects me . . . If a junior corrects me, he might do so sympathetically, not without sympathy.

I would then say "Good!" to him and would not trouble him, and seeing [my offense] I would make amends for it.'

"It occurs, too, to one of middle standing . . . to a junior: 'An elder—and one of middle standing and a junior—should correct me. I should correct an elder . . . and seeing [my offense] I would make amends for it.' It is in this way that there is co-residency among the good, and it is in this way that the good live together."

(AN 2:62, NDB 168–70)

6. Accepting Correction from Others

[Venerable Mahāmoggallāna is addressing the monks:] "Friends, though a monk asks thus: 'Let the venerable ones correct me, I need to be corrected by the venerable ones,' yet if he is difficult to correct and possesses qualities that make him difficult to correct, if he is impatient and does not take instruction rightly, then his fellow monks think that he should not be corrected or instructed, and they think of him as a person not to be trusted.

"What qualities make him difficult to correct? (1) Here a monk has evil desires and is dominated by evil desires; this is a quality that makes him difficult to correct. (2) Again, a monk lauds himself and disparages others; this is a quality that makes him difficult to correct. (3) Again, a monk is angry and is overcome by anger . . . (4) . . . angry and resentful because of anger . . . (5) . . . angry and stubborn because of anger . . . (6) . . . angry, and he utters words bordering on anger . . . (7) Again, when reproved, he resists the reprover . . . (8) . . . when reproved, he denigrates the reprover . . . (9) . . . when reproved, he counter-reproves the reprover . . . (10) . . . when reproved, he prevaricates, leads the talk aside, and shows anger, hate, and bitterness . . . (11) . . . when reproved, he fails to account for his conduct. . . . (12) Again, a monk is contemptuous and insolent . . . (13) . . . envious and miserly . . . (14) . . . fraudulent and deceitful . . . (15) . . . obstinate and arrogant. . . . (16) Again, a monk adheres to his own views, holds to them tenaciously, and relinquishes them with difficulty; this is a quality that makes him difficult to correct. These are called the qualities that make him difficult to correct.

"Friends, though a monk does not ask thus: 'Let the venerable ones correct me; I need to be corrected by the venerable ones,' yet if he is easy to correct and possesses qualities that make him easy to correct, if he is patient and takes instruction rightly, then his fellow monks think that he should be corrected and instructed, and they think of him as a person to be trusted.

"What qualities make him easy to correct? (1) Here a monk has no evil desires and is not dominated by evil desires; this is a quality that makes him easy to correct. (2) Again, a monk does not laud himself or disparage others; this is a quality. . . . (3) Again, a monk is not angry and overcome by anger . . . (4) . . . is not angry and resentful because of anger . . . (5) . . . is not angry and stubborn because of anger . . . (6) . . . is not angry, and he does not utter words bordering on anger . . . (7) Again, when reproved, he does not resist the reprover . . . (8) . . . when reproved, he does not denigrate the reprover . . . (9) . . . when reproved, he does not counter-reprove the reprover . . . (10) . . . when reproved, he does not prevaricate, lead the talk aside, and show anger, hate, and bitterness . . . (11) . . . when reproved, he accounts for his conduct . . . (12) Again, a monk is not contemptuous and insolent . . . (13) . . . not envious and miserly . . . (14) . . . not fraudulent and deceitful . . . (15) . . . not obstinate and arrogant . . . (16) Again, a monk does not adhere to his own views and hold to them tenaciously, but relinquishes them easily; this is a quality that makes him easy to correct. Friends, these are called the qualities that make him easy to correct.

"Now, friends, a monk ought to infer about himself in the following way: (1) 'A person with evil desires and dominated by evil desires is displeasing and disagreeable to me. If I were to have evil desires and be dominated by evil desires, I would be displeasing and disagreeable to others.' A monk who knows this should arouse his mind thus: 'I shall not have evil desires and be dominated by evil desires.'

(2) "'A person who lauds himself and disparages others . . . (16) 'A person who adheres to his own views, holds to them tenaciously, and relinquishes them with difficulty is displeasing and disagreeable to me. If I were to adhere to my own views, hold to them tenaciously, and relinquish them with difficulty, I would be displeasing and disagreeable to others.' A monk who knows this should arouse his mind thus: 'I shall not adhere to my own views, hold on to them tenaciously, but I shall relinquish them easily.'

"Now, friends, a monk should review himself thus: (1) 'Do I have evil desires and am I dominated by evil desires?' If, when he reviews himself, he knows: 'I have evil desires, I am dominated by evil desires,' then he should make an effort to abandon those evil unwholesome qualities. But if, when he reviews himself, he knows: 'I have no evil desires, I am not dominated by evil desires,' then he can abide happy and glad, training day and night in wholesome qualities.

(2) "Again, a monk should review himself thus: 'Do I praise myself and disparage others?' . . . (16) 'Do I adhere to my own views, hold on to them tenaciously, and relinquish them with difficulty?' If, when he reviews himself, he knows: 'I adhere to my own views . . . ,' then he should make an effort to abandon those evil unwholesome qualities. But if, when he reviews himself, he knows: 'I do not adhere to my own views . . . ,' then he can abide happy and glad, training day and night in wholesome qualities.

"Friends, when a monk reviews himself thus, if he sees that these evil unwholesome qualities are not all abandoned in himself, then he should make an effort to abandon them all. But if, when he reviews himself thus, he sees that they are all abandoned in himself, then he can abide happy and glad, training day and night in wholesome qualities. Just as when a young woman, fond of ornaments, on viewing the image of her own face in a clear bright mirror or in a basin of clear water, sees a smudge or a blemish on it, she makes an effort to remove it, but if she sees no smudge or blemish on it, she becomes glad thus: 'It is a gain for me that it is clean'; so too when a monk reviews himself thus . . . then he can abide happy and glad, training day and night in wholesome qualities."

(MN 15, MLDB 190–93)

7. Settling Disputes between Laity and Sangha

(1) Overturning the Almsbowl

"Monks, when a lay follower possesses eight qualities, the Sangha, if it so wishes, may overturn the almsbowl on him. What eight? (1) He tries to prevent monks from acquiring gains; (2) he tries to bring harm to monks; (3) he tries to prevent monks from residing [nearby]; (4) he insults and reviles monks; (5) he divides monks from each other; (6) he speaks dispraise of the Buddha; (7) he speaks dispraise of the Dhamma; (8) he speaks dispraise of the Sangha. When a lay follower possesses these eight qualities, the Sangha, if it so wishes, may overturn the almsbowl on him.

"Monks, when a lay follower possesses eight qualities, the Sangha, if it so wishes, may turn the almsbowl upright on him. What eight? (1) He does not try to prevent monks from acquiring gains; (2) he does not try to bring harm to monks; (3) he does not try to prevent monks from residing [nearby]; (4) he does not insult and revile monks; (5) he does not divide monks from each other; (6) he speaks praise of the Buddha; (7) he speaks praise of the Dhamma; (8) he speaks praise of the Sangha. When a lay follower possesses these eight qualities, the Sangha, if it so wishes, may turn the almsbowl upright on him."

(AN 8:87, NDB 1235)

(2) Loss of Confidence

"Monks, when a monk possesses eight qualities, lay followers, if they wish, may proclaim their loss of confidence in him.[8] What eight? (1) He tries to prevent laypeople from acquiring gains; (2) he tries to bring harm to laypeople; (3) he insults and reviles laypeople; (4) he divides laypeople from each other; (5) he speaks dispraise of the Buddha; (6) he speaks dispraise of the Dhamma; (7) he speaks dispraise of the Sangha; (8) they see him at an improper resort. When a monk possesses these eight qualities, lay followers, if they wish, may proclaim their loss of confidence in him.

"Monks, when a monk possesses eight qualities, lay followers, if they wish, may restore their confidence in him. What eight? (1) He does not try to prevent laypeople from acquiring gains; (2) he does not try to bring harm to laypeople; (3) he does not insult and revile laypeople; (4) he does not divide laypeople from each other; (5) he speaks praise of the Buddha; (6) he speaks praise of the Dhamma; (7) he speaks praise of the Sangha; (8) they see him at a [proper] resort. When a monk possesses these eight qualities, lay followers, if they wish, may restore their confidence in him."

(AN 8:88, NDB 1236)

(3) Reconciliation

"Monks, when a monk possesses eight qualities, the Sangha, if it wishes, may enjoin an act of reconciliation on him.[9] What eight? (1) He tries to prevent laypeople from acquiring gains; (2) he tries to bring harm to laypeople; (3) he insults and reviles laypeople; (4) he divides laypeople from each other; (5) he speaks dispraise of the Buddha; (6) he speaks dispraise of the Dhamma; (7) he speaks dispraise of the Sangha; (8) he does not fulfill a legitimate promise to laypeople. When a monk possesses these eight qualities, the Sangha, if it wishes, may enjoin an act of reconciliation on him.

"Monks, when a monk possesses eight qualities, the Sangha, if it wishes, may revoke an act of reconciliation [previously imposed on him]. What eight? (1) He does not try to prevent laypeople from acquiring gains; (2) he does not try to bring harm to laypeople; (3) he does not insult and revile laypeople; (4) he does not divide laypeople from each other; (5) he speaks praise of the Buddha; (6) he speaks praise of the Dhamma; (7) he speaks praise of the Sangha; (8) he fulfills a legitimate promise to laypeople. When a monk possesses these eight qualities, the Sangha, if it wishes, may revoke an act of reconciliation [previously imposed on him]."

(AN 8:89, NDB 1236–37)

8. Expelling Miscreants

(1) Sweep the Chaff Away!

On one occasion the Blessed One was dwelling at Campā on a bank of the Gaggārā Lotus Pond. Now on that occasion monks were reproving a monk for an offense. When being reproved, that monk answered evasively, diverted the discussion to an irrelevant subject, and displayed anger, hatred, and resentment. Then the Blessed One addressed the monks: "Monks, eject this person! Monks, eject this person! This person should be banished. Why should another's son vex you?[10]

"Here, monks, so long as the monks do not see his offense, a certain person has the same deportment as the good monks. When, however, they see his offense, they know him as a corruption among ascetics, just chaff and trash among ascetics. Then they expel him. For what reason? So that he doesn't corrupt the good monks.

"Suppose that when a field of barley is growing, some blighted barley would appear that would be just chaff and trash among the barley. As long as its head has not come forth, its roots would be just like that of the good barley; its stem would be just like that of the good barley; its leaves would be just like those of the good barley. When, however, its head comes forth, they know it as blighted barley, just chaff and trash among the barley. Then they pull it up by the root and cast it out from the barley field. For what reason? So that it doesn't spoil the good barley.

"So too, so long as the monks do not see his offense, a certain person here has the same deportment as the good monks. When, however, they see his offense, they know him as a corruption among ascetics, just chaff and trash among ascetics. Then they expel him. For what reason? So that he doesn't corrupt the good monks."

> By living together with him, know him as
> an angry person with evil desires;
> a denigrator, obstinate, and insolent,
> envious, miserly, and deceptive.
>
> He speaks to people just like an ascetic,
> [addressing them] with a calm voice;
> but secretly he does evil deeds,
> holds pernicious views, and lacks respect.
>
> Though he is devious, a speaker of lies,
> you should know him as he truly is;
> then you should all meet in harmony
> and firmly drive him away.
>
> Get rid of the trash!
> Remove the depraved fellows!
> Sweep the chaff away, non-ascetics
> who think themselves ascetics!
>
> Having banished those of evil desires,
> of bad conduct and resort,
> dwell in communion, ever mindful,
> the pure with the pure;

then, in harmony, alert,
you will make an end of suffering.

(AN 8:10, NDB 1122–24)

(2) Forced Eviction

On one occasion the Blessed One was dwelling at Sāvatthī in Migāramātā's Mansion in the Eastern Park. Now on that occasion, on the day of the *uposatha*, the Blessed One was sitting surrounded by the Sangha of monks. Then, as the night advanced, when the first watch passed, the Venerable Ānanda rose from his seat, arranged his upper robe over one shoulder, reverently saluted the Blessed One, and said to him: "Bhante, the night has advanced; the first watch has passed; the Sangha has been sitting for a long time. Let the Blessed One recite the Pātimokkha to the monks." When this was said, the Blessed One was silent.

As the night advanced [still further], when the middle watch passed, the Venerable Ānanda rose from his seat a second time, arranged his upper robe over one shoulder, reverently saluted the Blessed One, and said to him: "Bhante, the night has advanced [still further]; the middle watch has passed; the Sangha has been sitting for a long time. Bhante, let the Blessed One recite the Pātimokkha to the monks." A second time the Blessed One was silent.

As the night advanced [still further], when the last watch passed, when dawn arrived and a rosy tint appeared on the horizon, the Venerable Ānanda rose from his seat a third time, arranged his upper robe over one shoulder, reverently saluted the Blessed One, and said to him: "Bhante, the night has advanced [still further]; the last watch has passed; dawn has arrived and a rosy tint has appeared on the horizon; the Sangha has been sitting for a long time. Let the Blessed One recite the Pātimokkha to the monks."

"This assembly, Ānanda, is impure."

Then it occurred to the Venerable Mahāmoggallāna: "What person was the Blessed One referring to when he said: 'This assembly is impure'?" Then the Venerable Mahāmoggallāna fixed his attention on the entire Sangha of monks, encompassing their minds with his own mind. He then saw that person sitting in the midst of the Sangha: one who was immoral, of bad character, impure, of suspect behavior, secretive in his actions, not an ascetic though claiming to be one, not a celibate though claiming to be one, inwardly rotten, corrupt, depraved. Having seen him, he rose from his seat, went up to that person, and said to him: "Get up, friend. The Blessed One has seen you. You cannot live in communion with the monks." When this was said, that person remained silent.

A second time . . . A third time the Venerable Mahāmoggallāna said to that person: "Get up, friend. The Blessed One has seen you. You cannot live in communion with the monks." A third time that person remained silent.

Then the Venerable Mahāmoggallāna grabbed that person by the arm, evicted him through the outer gatehouse, and bolted the door. Then he returned to the Blessed One and said to him: "I have evicted that person, Bhante. The assembly is pure. Let the Blessed One recite the Pātimokkha to the monks."

"It's astounding and amazing, Moggallāna, how that hollow man waited until he was grabbed by the arm." Then the Blessed One addressed the monks: "Now, monks, you yourselves should conduct the *uposatha* and recite the Pātimokkha. From today onward, I will no longer do so. It is impossible and inconceivable that the Tathāgata could conduct the *uposatha* and recite the Pātimokkha in an impure assembly."

(from AN 8:20, NDB 1145–46; Ud 5.5)

X. Establishing an Equitable Society

Introduction

In the last part of this anthology, we move from the intentional community to the natural community, proceeding from the family to the larger society and then to the state. The texts included here reveal the pragmatic astuteness of the Buddha's wisdom, his ability to address practical issues with uncanny insight and directness. Although he had adopted the life of a *samaṇa*, a renunciant who stood outside all social institutions, from the distance he looked back into the social institutions of his time and suggested ideals and arrangements to promote the spiritual, psychological, and physical well-being of people still immersed in the confines of the world. He apparently saw the key to a healthy society to lie in the fulfillment of one's responsibilities toward others. He regarded the social order as a tapestry of overlapping and intersecting relationships each of which imposed on people duties with respect to those at the other pole of each relationship in which they participated.

This point comes through most saliently in **Text X,1**, an excerpt from a discourse given to a young man named Sīgalaka. The Buddha here treats society as constituted by six paired relationships: parents and children, husbands and wives, friends with each other, employers and employees, teachers and students, and religious teachers and lay supporters. For each the Buddha proposed five (or in one case six) duties that each should fulfill toward the others. He sees the individual—every individual—as standing at a point where the "six directions" converge, and thus obliged to honor these directions by performing the duties inherent in the relationship.

The Buddha regarded the family as the basic unit of social integration and acculturation. It is especially the close, loving relationship between parents and children that nurtures the virtues and sense of humane responsibility essential to a cohesive social order. Within the family, these values are transmitted from one generation to the next, and thus a harmonious society is highly dependent on cordial and respectful relations between parents and children. In **Text X,2(1)** he explains how parents are of great benefit to their children, and in **X,2(2)** he says that one's parents can never be adequately repaid by conferring material benefits on them but only by establishing them in faith, virtuous conduct, generosity, and wisdom. Wholesome relations between parents and children depend in turn on the mutual affection and respect of husband and wife. The discourse selected for **Text X,3** offers guidelines for proper relationships between married couples, holding that the ideal marriage is one in which both husband and wife share a commitment to virtuous conduct, generosity, and spiritual values.

In the next section I have collected texts that deal with the social behavior of the householder. The first two, **Texts X,4(1)–(2)**, affirm that the devout householder arises for the welfare of many and leads his family members in the development of faith, virtue, learning, generosity, and wisdom. **Text X,4(3)** discusses the proper ways of seeking wealth, which must take place within the strictures of right livelihood. The spiritual dimension enters by asserting that the householder uses wealth "without being tied to it, infatuated with it, and blindly absorbed in it." **Text X,4(4)** speaks of five trades that are prohibited for the earnest lay disciple, prohibited because they involve harm, either actual or potential, for other living beings. **Text X,4(5)** then explains five proper ways of using wealth. The explanation shows that wealth rightly earned is to be used for both self-benefit and the benefit of others; after one has secured the well-being of oneself and one's family, one is to use the wealth primarily to perform meritorious deeds that are of service to others.

The next section brings us back to the issue of caste, touched on from a monastic perspective in Part VII. Contrary to a common belief, the Buddha did not openly advocate for the abolition of the caste system, which in his time had not yet acquired the complexity and rigidity it acquired in later centuries, primarily as formulated in the Hindu law books. Perhaps he saw that social divisions and the different responsibilities they entailed were inevitable. But he did reject claims about the sanctity of the caste system on several grounds, theological, moral, and spiritual. Theologically, he repudiated the brahmin claim that the castes were created by Brahmā, the creator god; instead he regarded the system as a mere social institution of purely human origin. Morally, he rejected the belief that caste status was indicative of moral worth, with superior moral status inhering in those of the higher castes. Instead he held that it was one's deeds that determined one's moral worth, and that anyone from any social class who engaged in unwholesome deeds would lower their moral status and anyone who engaged in wholesome deeds would elevate their moral status. And spiritually, as we saw earlier, he held that anyone from any caste could practice the Dhamma and attain the ultimate goal.

These arguments are presented here in **Texts X,5(1)–(4)**. The conversations recorded in these discourses—in which the caste structure is treated as a model the brahmins seek to impose on society—suggest that in northeast India, where Buddhism arose, caste stratification had not reached the degree of rigidity and authoritativeness that it may have reached in western and central India. It is also interesting to note that when listing the castes in sequence, where the brahmins put themselves on top and the khattiyas beneath them, the Buddha puts the khattiyas on top and the brahmins in second place. In this respect, he may have been following the convention that prevailed in the northeastern states of the subcontinent.

In **X,5(1)** the Buddha argues against the brahmin claim, advanced by the brahmin Esukārī, that society should be ordered according to a fixed hierarchy of service, such that everyone in the lower castes must serve the brahmins, while the suddas, at the bottom of the caste ladder, must serve everyone else. The Buddha, in contrast, holds that service should be based on the opportunities offered for one's moral advancement. The brahmin Esukārī also maintains that those in each caste have their own fixed duty that follows from their caste status; this seems to be a precursor of the theory of *svadharma* that became prominent in the Hindu law books, the idea that each caste has its own duties that one must fulfill if one is to reap a better rebirth and progress toward final liberation. Again, the Buddha rejects this view, holding that the "supramundane Dhamma" is the natural wealth of every person. Whoever observes the principles of good conduct, regardless of caste background, is cultivating "the Dhamma that is wholesome."

In **Text X,5(2)**, the monk Mahākaccāna, who was himself of brahmin stock, argues against the brahmin claim that the caste system is of divine origins and that the brahmins alone are "the sons of Brahmā, the offspring of Brahmā." He maintains instead that "this is just a saying in the world." The caste system is purely conventional, and those from any caste may prove themselves morally worthy or morally defective. In **X,5(3)–(4)** the Buddha again rejects the idea that caste status is determined by birth and proposes redefinitions of the concepts of brahmin and outcast, respectively, whereby they are defined not by birth but by a person's own moral character.

The next section briefly looks at the Buddha's political vision. In his time, the Indian subcontinent was divided into sixteen states, which were of two types: tribal republics and monarchies. We already saw an example of the Buddha's advice to the republican leaders in **Text VII,3(4),** on the seven conditions for non-decline that he taught to the Vajjis. However, the northern region of India was rapidly undergoing a tectonic transition that was overturning the prevailing political order. The kingships of several states were expanding and swallowing up weaker kingdoms and the small republics, whose days seemed numbered. Competing claims for territory and wealth led to a rise in militarism and violent clashes. The region was rapidly heading toward an era of ruthless power struggles and vicious wars of aggression poignantly depicted in the following verse (SN 1:28, CDB 103):

> Those of great wealth and property,
> even khattiyas who rule the country,
> look at each other with greedy eyes,
> insatiable in sensual pleasures.

Since the triumph of the monarchical type of government appeared inevitable, the Buddha sought to safeguard against abuses of power by positing a model of kingship that would subordinate the king to a higher authority, an objective standard of goodness that could curb the arbitrary exercise of power. He realized that in a monarchical political system, the whole society follows the example set by its ruler, whether for good or bad. Thus in **Text X,6(1)** he describes the role of the king, ascribing an almost mystical potency to the influence of the ruler's conduct on his realm. In an age of military struggles over territory, he condemned the resort to war as a means of resolving conflicts. **Text X,6(2)** states that victory only breeds enmity and maintains the cycle of retaliation. The Jātakas, the stories of the Buddha's past lives, further summarize the qualities expected in a righteous ruler with a scheme of ten royal virtues: giving, moral conduct, relinquishment, honesty, gentleness, personal austerity, non-anger, non-injury, patience, and non-opposition to the will of the people.[1] The Kukka Jātaka, for example, describes the virtuous king as one who "following these ten royal virtues, ruling in accordance with the Dhamma, brings about prosperity and progress for himself and others without troubling anyone" (Jātakas III 320).

To ensure that kings had an exemplary standard of rulership to emulate, the Buddha established the ideal of the "wheel-turning monarch" (*rājā cakkavattī*), the righteous king who rules in compliance with the Dhamma, the impersonal law of righteousness. The wheel-turning monarch is the secular counterpart of the Buddha; for both, the wheel is the symbol of their authority. As **Text X,6(3)** shows, the Dhamma that the wheel-turning monarch obeys is the ethical justification for his rule. He extends protection to all in his realm, to people from every walk of life and even to the birds and beasts. Symbolized by the sacred wheel-treasure, the law of righteousness enables the king to peaceably conquer the world and establish a universal reign of peace based on observance of the five precepts and the ten courses of wholesome action, as described in **Text X,6(4)**.

Among the monarch's duties is to prevent crime from proliferating in his kingdom, and to keep the kingdom safe from crime he must give wealth to those in need. In Early Buddhism, poverty is regarded as the breeding ground of criminality and the alleviation of poverty thus becomes one of the royal duties. This duty is mentioned among the obligations of a wheel-turning monarch in **Text X,6(5)**, which shows how, from the failure to alleviate poverty, all manner of moral depravities arise: theft, murder, lying, and other transgressions. The king's obligation to relieve poverty is elaborated in **X,6(6)**. Here, in a story purportedly referring to the distant past, a wise chaplain—who is none other than the Buddha in a previous birth—advises the king that the proper way to end the theft and brigandage plaguing his realm is not by imposing harsher punishments and stricter law enforcement but by giving the citizens the means they need to earn a decent living. Once the people enjoy a satisfactory standard of living, they lose all interest in harming others and the country enjoys peace and tranquility.

X. Establishing an Equitable Society

1. Reciprocal Responsibilities

[The Buddha is speaking to a young man named Sīgalaka:] "And how, young man, does the noble disciple protect the six directions? These six things are to be regarded as the six directions. The east denotes mother and father. The south denotes teachers. The west denotes wife and children. The north denotes friends and companions. The nadir denotes servants, workers, and helpers. The zenith denotes ascetics and brahmins.

"There are five ways in which a son should minister to his mother and father as the eastern direction. [He should think:] 'Having been supported by them, I will support them. I will perform their duties for them. I will keep up the family tradition. I will be worthy of my heritage. After my parents' deaths I will distribute gifts on their behalf.' And there are five ways in which the parents, so ministered to by their son as the eastern direction, will reciprocate: they will restrain him from evil, support him in doing good, teach him some skill, find him a suitable wife, and, in due time, hand over his inheritance to him. In this way the eastern direction is covered, making it secure and free from peril.

"There are five ways in which pupils should minister to their teachers as the southern direction: by rising to greet them, by waiting on them, by being attentive, by serving them, by mastering the skills they teach. And there are five ways in which their teachers, thus ministered to by their pupils as the southern direction, will reciprocate: they will give thorough instruction, make sure they have grasped what they should have duly grasped, give them a thorough grounding in all skills, recommend them to their friends and colleagues, and provide them with security in all directions. In this way the southern direction is covered, making it secure and free from peril.

"There are five ways in which a husband should minister to his wife as the western direction: by honoring her, by not disparaging her, by not being unfaithful to her, by giving authority to her, by providing her with adornments. And there are five ways in which a wife, thus ministered to by her husband as the western direction, will reciprocate: by properly organizing her work, by being kind to the servants, by not being unfaithful, by protecting stores, and by being skillful and diligent in all she has to do. In this way the western direction is covered, making it secure and free from peril.

"There are five ways in which a man should minister to his friends and companions as the northern direction: by gifts, by kindly words, by looking after their welfare, by treating them like himself, and by keeping his word. And there are five ways in which friends and companions, thus ministered to by a man as the northern direction, will reciprocate: by looking after him when he is inattentive, by looking after his property when he is inattentive, by being a refuge when he is afraid, by not deserting him when he is in trouble, and by showing concern for his children. In this way the northern direction is covered, making it secure and free from peril.

"There are five ways in which a master should minister to his servants and workers as the nadir: by arranging their work according to their strength, by supplying them with food and wages, by looking after them when they are ill, by sharing special delicacies with them, and by letting them off work at the right time. And there are five ways in which servants and workers, thus ministered to by their master as the nadir, will reciprocate: they will get up before him, go to bed after him, take only what they are given, do their work properly, and be bearers of his praise and good repute. In this way the nadir is covered, making it secure and free from peril.

"There are five ways in which a man should minister to ascetics and brahmins as the zenith: by kindness in bodily deed, speech, and thought, by keeping open house for them, and by supplying their bodily needs. And the ascetics and brahmins, thus ministered to by him as the zenith, will reciprocate in six ways: they will restrain him from evil, enjoin him in the good, be compassionate toward him, teach him what he has not learned, clarify what he has learned, and point out to him the way to heaven. In this way the zenith is covered, making it secure and free from peril."

(from DN 31, LDB 466–68)

2. Parents and Children

(1) Parents Are of Great Help

"Monks, those families dwell with Brahmā where at home the parents are respected by their children. Those families dwell with the ancient teachers where at home the parents are respected by their children. Those families dwell with the ancient deities where at home the parents are respected by the children. Those families dwell with the holy ones where at home the parents are respected by their children.

"'Brahmā,' monks, is a term for father and mother. 'The ancient teachers' is a term for father and mother. 'The ancient deities' is a term for father and mother. 'The holy ones' is a term for father and mother. And why? Parents are of great help to their children; they bring them up, feed them, and show them the world."

(AN 4:63, NDB 453)

(2) Repaying One's Parents

"Monks, I declare that there are two persons that are not easily repaid. What two? One's mother and father. Even if one should carry about one's mother on one shoulder and one's father on the other, and while doing so should live a hundred years, reach the age of a hundred years; and if one should attend to them by anointing them with balms, by massaging, bathing, and rubbing their limbs, and they should even void their excrements there—even by that one would not do enough for one's parents, nor would one repay them. Even if one were to establish one's parents as the supreme lords and rulers over this earth so rich in the seven treasures, one would not do enough for them, nor would one repay them. For what reason? Parents are of great help to their children; they bring them up, feed them, and show them the world. But one who encourages his unbelieving parents, settles and establishes them in faith; who encourages his immoral parents, settles and establishes them in moral virtue; who encourages his miserly parents, settles and establishes them in generosity; who encourages his ignorant parents, settles and establishes them in wisdom—such a one does enough for his parents: he repays them and more than repays them for what they have done."

(AN 2:33, NDB 153–54)

3. Husbands and Wives

On one occasion the Blessed One was traveling along the highway between Madhurā and Verañjā, and a number of householders and their wives were traveling along the same road. Then the Blessed One left the road and sat down on a seat at the foot of a tree. The householders and their wives saw the Blessed One sitting there and approached him. Having paid homage to him, they sat down to one side, and the Blessed One then said to them:

"Householders, there are these four kinds of marriages. What four? A wretch lives together with a wretch; a wretch lives together with a goddess; a god lives together with a wretch; a god lives together with a goddess.

"And how does a wretch live together with a wretch? Here, householders, the husband is one who destroys life, takes what is not given, engages in sexual misconduct, speaks falsely, and indulges in wines, liquor, and intoxicants, the basis for negligence; he is immoral, of bad character; he dwells at home with a heart obsessed by the stain of miserliness; he abuses and reviles ascetics and brahmins. And his wife is exactly the same in all respects. It is in such a way that a wretch lives together with a wretch.

"And how does a wretch live together with a goddess? Here, householders, the husband is one who destroys life . . . who abuses and reviles ascetics and brahmins. But his wife is one who abstains from the destruction of life . . . from wines, liquor, and intoxicants; she is virtuous, of good character; she dwells at home with a heart free from the stain of miserliness; she does not abuse or revile ascetics and brahmins. It is in such a way that a wretch lives together with a goddess.

"And how does a god live together with a wretch? Here, householders, the husband is one who abstains from the destruction of life . . . who does not abuse or revile ascetics and brahmins. But his wife is one who destroys life . . . who abuses and reviles ascetics and brahmins. It is in such a way that a god lives together with a wretch.

"And how does a god live together with a goddess? Here, householders, the husband is one who abstains from the destruction of life . . . from wines, liquor, and intoxicants; he is virtuous, of good character; he dwells at home with a heart free from the stain of miserliness; he does not abuse or revile ascetics and brahmins. And his wife is exactly the same in all respects. It is in such a way that a god lives together with a goddess.

"These, householders, are the four kinds of marriages."

(AN 4:53, NDB 443–44)

4. The Household

(1) For the Welfare of Many

"Monks, when a good person is born in a family, it is for the good, welfare, and happiness of many people. It is for the good, welfare, and happiness of (1) his mother and father, (2) his wife and children, (3) his servants, workers, and helpers, (4) his friends and companions, and (5) ascetics and brahmins. Just as a great rain cloud, nurturing all the crops, appears for the good, welfare, and happiness of many people, so too, when a good person is born in a family, it is for the good, welfare, and happiness of many people. It is for the good, welfare, and happiness of his mother and father . . . ascetics and brahmins."

(AN 5:42, NDB 667)

(2) Like the Himalayas

"Monks, based on the Himalayas, the king of mountains, great sal trees grow in five ways. What five? (1) They grow in branches, leaves, and foliage; (2) they grow in bark; (3) they grow in shoots; (4) they grow in softwood; and (5) they grow in heartwood. Based on the Himalayas, the king of mountains, great sal trees grow in these five ways. So too, when the family head is endowed with faith, the people in the family who depend on him grow in five ways. What five? (1) They grow in faith; (2) they grow in virtuous behavior; (3) they grow in learning; (4) they grow in generosity; and (5) they grow in wisdom. When the head of a family is endowed with faith, the people in the family who depend on him grow in these five ways."

(AN 5:40, NDB 664)

(3) Ways of Seeking Wealth

"The householder who seeks wealth righteously, without violence, and makes himself happy and pleased, and shares it and does meritorious deeds, and uses that wealth without being tied to it, infatuated with it, and blindly absorbed in it, seeing the danger in it and understanding the escape—he may be praised on four grounds. The first ground on which he may be praised is that he seeks wealth righteously, without violence. The second ground on which he may be praised is that he makes himself happy and pleased. The third ground on which he may be praised is that he shares the wealth and does meritorious deeds. The fourth ground on which he may be praised is that he uses that wealth without being tied to it, infatuated with it, and blindly absorbed in it, seeing the danger in it and understanding the escape. This householder may be praised on these four grounds.

"Just as from a cow comes milk, from milk curd, from curd butter, from butter ghee, and from ghee comes cream-of-ghee, which is reckoned the foremost of all these, so among all householders, the foremost, the best, the preeminent, the supreme, and the finest is the one who seeks wealth righteously, without violence; and having done so, makes himself happy and pleased; and shares the wealth and does meritorious deeds; and uses that wealth without being tied to it, infatuated with it, and blindly absorbed in it, seeing the danger in it and understanding the escape."

(from AN 10:91, NDB 1461; see too SN 42:12, CDB 1356)

(4) Avoiding Wrong Livelihood

"Monks, a lay follower should not engage in these five trades. What five? Trading in weapons, trading in living beings, trading in meat, trading in intoxicants, and trading in poisons. A lay follower should not engage in these five trades."

(AN 5:177, NDB 790)

(5) The Proper Use of Wealth

The Blessed One said to the householder Anāthapiṇḍika: "Householder, there are these five utilizations of wealth. What are the five?

(1) "Here, householder, with wealth acquired by energetic striving, amassed by the strength of his arms, earned by the sweat of his brow, righteous wealth righteously gained, the noble disciple makes himself happy and pleased and properly maintains himself in happiness; he makes his parents happy and pleased and properly maintains them in happiness; he makes his wife and children, his servants, workers, and helpers happy and pleased and properly maintains them in happiness. This is the first utilization of wealth.

(2) "Again, with wealth acquired by energetic striving . . . righteously gained, the noble disciple makes his friends and companions happy and pleased and properly maintains them in happiness. This is the second utilization of wealth.

(3) "Again, with wealth acquired by energetic striving . . . righteously gained, the noble disciple makes provisions with his wealth against the losses that might arise because of fire or floods, kings or bandits or unloved heirs; he makes himself secure against them. This is the third utilization of wealth.

(4) "Again, with wealth acquired by energetic striving . . . righteously gained, the noble disciple makes the five oblations: to relatives, guests, ancestors, the king, and the deities. This is the fourth utilization of wealth.

(5) "Again, with wealth acquired by energetic striving . . . righteously gained, the noble disciple establishes an uplifting offering of alms—an offering that is heavenly, resulting in happiness, conducive to heaven—to those ascetics and brahmins who refrain from intoxication and heedlessness, who are settled in patience and mildness, who tame themselves, calm themselves, and train themselves for nibbāna. This is the fifth utilization of wealth."

(AN 5:41, NDB 665–66)

5. SOCIAL STATUS

(1) No Fixed Hierarchy of Privilege

Then the brahmin Esukārī went to the Blessed One and said to him: "Master Gotama, the brahmins prescribe four levels of service. They prescribe the level of service toward a brahmin, the level of service toward a khattiya, the level of service toward a vessa, and the level of service toward a sudda. The brahmins prescribe this as the level of service toward a brahmin: a brahmin may serve a brahmin, a khattiya may serve a brahmin, a vessa may serve a brahmin, and a sudda may serve a brahmin. They prescribe this as the level of service toward a khattiya: a khattiya may serve a khattiya, a vessa may serve a khattiya, and a sudda may serve a khattiya. They prescribe this as the level of service toward a vessa: a vessa may serve a vessa and a sudda may serve a vessa. They prescribe this as the level of service toward a sudda: only a sudda may serve a sudda; for who else could serve a sudda? What does Master Gotama say about this?"

"Well, brahmin, has all the world authorized the brahmins to prescribe these four levels of service?" – "No, Master Gotama." – "Suppose, brahmin, they were to force a cut of meat upon a poor, penniless, destitute man and tell him: 'Good man, you must eat this meat and pay for it'; so too, without the consent of those [other] ascetics and brahmins, the brahmins nevertheless prescribe those four levels of service.

"I do not say, brahmin, that all are to be served, nor do I say that none are to be served. For if, when serving someone, one becomes worse and not better because of that service, then I say that he should not be served. And if, when serving someone, one becomes better and not worse because of that service, then I say that he should be served. . . .

"I do not say, brahmin, that one is better because one is from an aristocratic family, nor do I say that one is worse because one is from an aristocratic family. I do not say that one is better because one is of great beauty, nor do I say that one is worse because one is of great beauty. I do not say that one is better because one is of great wealth, nor do I say that one is worse because one is of great wealth. For one from an aristocratic family may destroy life, take what is not given, engage in sexual misconduct, speak falsely, speak divisively, speak harshly, gossip, be covetous, have a mind of ill will, and hold wrong view. Therefore I do not say that one is better because one is from an aristocratic family. But also one from an aristocratic family may abstain from destroying life, from taking what is not given, from sexual misconduct, from false speech, from divisive speech, from harsh speech, and from idle chatter, and he may be uncovetous, have a benevolent mind, and hold right view. Therefore I do not say that one is worse because one is from an aristocratic family.

"I do not say, brahmin, that all are to be served, nor do I say that none are to be served. For if, when serving someone, one's faith, virtue, learning, generosity, and wisdom increase in his service, then I say that he should be served."

The brahmin Esukārī next said to the Blessed One: "Master Gotama, the brahmins prescribe four types of wealth: the wealth of a brahmin, the wealth of a khattiya, the wealth of a vessa, and the wealth of a sudda. The brahmins prescribe wandering for alms as the wealth of a brahmin; a brahmin who spurns wandering for alms abuses his duty like a guard who takes what has not been given. They prescribe the bow and quiver as the wealth of a khattiya; a khattiya who spurns the bow and quiver abuses his duty like a guard who takes what has not been given. They prescribe agriculture and cattle-breeding as the wealth of a vessa; a vessa who spurns farming and cattle-breeding abuses his duty like a guard who takes what has not been given. They prescribe the sickle and carrying-pole as the wealth of a sudda; a sudda who spurns the sickle and carrying-pole abuses his duty like a guard who takes what has not been given. What does Master Gotama say about this?"

"Well, brahmin, has all the world authorized the brahmins to prescribe these four types of wealth?" – "No, Master Gotama." – "Suppose, brahmin, they were to force a cut of meat upon a poor, penniless, destitute man and tell him: 'Good man, you must eat this meat and pay for it'; so too, without the consent of those [other] ascetics and brahmins, the brahmins nevertheless prescribe these four types of wealth.

"Brahmin, I declare the noble supramundane Dhamma as a person's own wealth. But recollecting his ancient maternal and paternal family lineage, he is reckoned according to wherever he is reborn. If he is reborn in a clan of khattiyas, he is reckoned as a khattiya; if he is reborn in a clan of brahmins, he is reckoned as a brahmin; if he is reborn in a clan of vessas, he is reckoned as a vessa; if he is reborn in a clan of suddas, he is reckoned as a sudda. Just as fire is reckoned by the particular condition dependent on which it burns—when fire burns dependent on logs, it is reckoned as a log fire; when fire burns dependent on faggots, it is reckoned as a faggot fire; when fire burns dependent on grass, it is reckoned as a grass fire; when fire burns dependent on cowdung, it is reckoned as a cowdung fire—so too, brahmin, I declare the noble supramundane Dhamma as a person's own wealth. But recollecting his ancient maternal and paternal lineage, he is reckoned according to wherever he is reborn."

(from MN 96, MLDB 786–89)

(2) Caste Is Mere Convention

King Avantiputta of Madhurā asked the Venerable Mahākaccāna: "Master Kaccāna, the brahmins say thus: 'Brahmins are the highest caste, those of any other caste are inferior; brahmins are the fairest caste, those of any other caste are dark; only brahmins are purified, not non-brahmins; brahmins alone are the sons of Brahmā, the offspring of Brahmā, born of his mouth, born of Brahmā, created by Brahmā, heirs of Brahmā.' What does Master Kaccāna say about that?"

"It is just a saying in the world, great king. And there is a way whereby it can be understood how that statement of the brahmins is just a saying in the world. What do you think, great king? If a khattiya prospers in wealth, will there be khattiyas who rise before him and retire after him, who are eager to serve him, who seek to please him and speak sweetly to him, and will there also be brahmins, vessas, and suddas who do likewise?" – "There will be, Master Kaccāna."

"What do you think, great king? If a brahmin prospers in wealth, will there be brahmins who rise before him and retire after him, who are eager to serve him, who seek to please him and speak sweetly to him, and will there also be vessas, suddas, and khattiyas who do likewise?" – "There will be, Master Kaccāna."

"What do you think, great king? If a vessa prospers in wealth, will there be vessas who rise before him and retire after him, who are eager to serve him, who seek to please him and speak sweetly to him, and will there also be suddas, khattiyas, and brahmins who do likewise?" – "There will be, Master Kaccāna."

"What do you think, great king? If a sudda prospers in wealth, will there be suddas who rise before him and retire after him, who are eager to serve him, who seek to please him and speak sweetly to him, and will there also be khattiyas, brahmins, and vessas who do likewise?" – "There will be, Master Kaccāna."

"What do you think, great king? If that is so, then are these four castes all the same, or are they not, or how does it appear to you in this case?"

"Surely if that is so, Master Kaccāna, then these four castes are all the same: there is no difference between them at all that I see."

"That is a way, great king, whereby it can be understood how that statement of the brahmins is just a saying in the world.

"What do you think, great king? Suppose a khattiya were to destroy life, take what is not given, engage in sexual misconduct, speak falsely, speak divisively, speak harshly, gossip, be covetous, have a mind of ill will, and hold wrong view. On the dissolution of the body, after death, would he be reborn in a state of misery, in a bad destination, in a lower world, in hell, or not, or how does it appear to you in this case?"

"He would be, Master Kaccāna. That is how it appears to me in this case, and thus I have heard from the arahants."

"Good, good, great king! What you think is good, great king, and what you have heard from the arahants is good. What do you think, great king? Suppose a brahmin . . . a vessa . . . a sudda were to act likewise?"

"If a brahmin . . . a vessa . . . a sudda were such, Master Kaccāna, he would be reborn in a state of misery, in a bad destination, in a lower world, in hell. That is how it appears to me in this case, and thus I have heard from the arahants."

"Good, good, great king! What you think is good, great king, and what you have heard from the arahants is good. What do you think, great king? If that is so, then are these four castes all the same, or are they not, or how does it appear to you in this case?"

"Surely if that is so, Master Kaccāna, then these four castes are all the same: there is no difference between them at all that I see."

"That is also a way, great king, whereby it can be understood how that statement of the brahmins is just a saying in the world.

"What do you think, great king? Suppose a khattiya were to abstain from the destruction of life, from taking what is not given, from sexual misconduct, from false speech, from divisive speech, from harsh speech, and from gossip, and were to be uncovetous, to have a benevolent mind, and to hold right view. On the dissolution of the body, after death, would he be reborn in a good destination, in the heavenly world, or not, or how does it appear to you in this case?"

"He would be, Master Kaccāna. That is how it appears to me in this case, and thus I have heard from the arahants."

"Good, good, great king! What you think is good, great king, and what you have heard from the arahants is good. What do you think, great king? Suppose a brahmin . . . a vessa . . . a sudda were to abstain from the destruction of life . . . and to hold right view. On the dissolution of the body, after death, would he be reborn in a good destination, in the heavenly world, or not, or how does it appear to you in this case?"

"He would be, Master Kaccāna. That is how it appears to me in this case, and thus I have heard from the arahants."

"Good, good, great king! What you think is good, great king, and what you have heard from the arahants is good. What do you think, great king? If that is so, then are these four castes all the same, or are they not, or how does it appear to you in this case?"

"Surely if that is so, Master Kaccāna, then these four castes are all the same: there is no difference between them at all that I see."

"That is also a way, great king, whereby it can be understood how that statement of the brahmins is just a saying in the world.

"What do you think, great king? Suppose a khattiya were to break into houses, plunder wealth, commit burglary, ambush highways, or seduce another's wife, and if your men arrested him and produced him, saying: 'Sire, this is the culprit; command what punishment for him you wish,' how would you treat him?"

"We would have him executed, Master Kaccāna, or we would have him fined, or we would have him exiled, or we would do with him as he deserved. Why is that? Because he has lost his former status of a khattiya and is simply reckoned as a robber."

"What do you think, great king? Suppose a brahmin . . . a vessa . . . a sudda were to do the same, and if your men arrested him and produced him, saying: 'Sire, this is the culprit; command what punishment for him you wish,' how would you treat him?"

"We would have him executed, Master Kaccāna, or we would have him fined, or we would have him exiled, or we would do with him as he deserved. Why is that? Because he has lost his former status of a brahmin . . . a vessa . . . a sudda and is simply reckoned as a robber."

"What do you think, great king? If that is so, then are these four castes all the same, or are they not, or how does it appear to you in this case?"

"Surely if that is so, Master Kaccāna, then these four castes are all the same; there is no difference between them at all that I see."

"That is also a way, great king, whereby it can be understood how that statement of the brahmins is just a saying in the world.

"What do you think, great king? Suppose a khattiya, having shaved off his hair and beard, put on the ocher robe, and gone forth from the home life into homelessness, were to abstain from the destruction of life, from taking what is not given, and from false speech. Refraining from eating at night, he would eat only in one part of the day, and would be celibate, virtuous, of good character. How would you treat him?"

"We would pay homage to him, Master Kaccāna, or we would rise up for him, or invite him to be seated; or we would invite him to accept robes, almsfood, lodgings, and medicinal requisites; or we would arrange for him lawful guarding, defense, and protection. Why is that? Because he has lost his former status of a khattiya and is simply reckoned as an ascetic."

"What do you think, great king? Suppose a brahmin . . . a vessa . . . a sudda were to do the same. How would you treat him?"

"We would pay homage to him, Master Kaccāna, or rise up for him, or invite him to be seated; or we would invite him to accept robes, almsfood, lodgings, and medicinal requisites; or we would arrange for him lawful guarding, defense, and protection. Why is that? Because he has lost his former status of a brahmin . . . a vessa . . . a sudda and is simply reckoned as an ascetic."

"What do you think, great king? If that is so, then are these four castes all the same, or are they not, or how does it appear to you in this case?"

"Surely if that is so, Master Kaccāna, then these four castes are all the same; there is no difference between them at all that I see."

"That is also a way, great king, whereby it can be understood how that statement of the brahmins is just a saying in the world."

(from MN 84, MLDB 698–702)

(3) Status Is Determined by Deeds

[The Buddha is speaking to the young brahmin Vāseṭṭha:]

"While among these many kinds of beings,
their distinctive marks are determined by birth,
among humans there are no distinctive marks
produced by their particular birth.

"Not by the hairs or the head,
not by the ears or by the eyes;
not by the mouth or the nose,
not by the lips or the brows;

"not by the neck or the shoulders,
not by the belly or the back;
not by the buttocks or the breast,
nor by the anus or genitals;

"not by the hands or the feet
nor by the fingers or nails;
not by the knees or the thighs,
nor by their color or voice:
birth does not make a distinctive mark
as it does for the other kinds of beings.

"In human beings with their bodies
nothing distinctive is found.
Classification among human beings
is spoken of by designation.

"The one among humans
who lives by husbandry,
you should know, Vāseṭṭha:
he is a farmer, not a brahmin.

"The one among humans
who earns his living by various crafts,
you should know, Vāseṭṭha:
he is a craftsman, not a brahmin.

"The one among humans
who lives by trade,

you should know, Vāseṭṭha:
he is a merchant, not a brahmin.

"The one among humans
who lives by serving others,
you should know, Vāseṭṭha:
he is a servant, not a brahmin.

"The one among humans
who lives by stealing,
you should know, Vāseṭṭha:
he is a thief, not a brahmin.

"The one among humans
who earns his living by archery,
you should know, Vāseṭṭha:
he is a warrior, not a brahmin.

"The one among humans
who lives by priestly service,
you should know, Vāseṭṭha:
he is a priest, not a brahmin.

"The one among humans
who rules over village and realm,
you should know, Vāseṭṭha:
he is a king, not a brahmin.

"I do not call someone a brahmin
based on genealogy and maternal origin.
He is just a pompous speaker
if he is impeded by things.
One who owns nothing, who takes nothing:
he is the one I call a brahmin.

"One who has cut off all fetters,
who is indeed not agitated,
who has overcome all ties, detached:
he is the one I call a brahmin. . . .

"One who knows his past abodes,
who sees heaven and the plane of misery,

who has reached the destruction of birth:
he is the one I call a brahmin.

"For the name and clan ascribed to one
is a designation in the world.
Having originated by convention,
it is ascribed here and there.

"For those who do not know this,
wrong view has long been their tendency.
Not knowing, they tell us:
'One is a brahmin by birth.'

"One is not a brahmin by birth,
nor by birth a non-brahmin.
By action one becomes a brahmin,
by action one becomes a non-brahmin.

"One becomes a farmer by action,
by action one becomes a craftsmen.
One becomes a merchant by action,
by action one becomes a servant.

"One becomes a thief by action,
by action one becomes a soldier.
One becomes a priest by action,
by action one becomes a king.

"So that is how the wise
see action as it really is—
seers of dependent origination,
skilled in action and its result.

"By action the world goes round,
by action the population goes round.
Sentient beings are fastened by action
like the linch pin of a moving chariot.

"By austerity, by the spiritual life,
by self-control, by inner taming—
by this one is a brahmin;
this is supreme brahminhood."

(from MN 98, MLDB 800–807; Sn III,9)

(4) Deeds Make the Outcast

The Blessed One said to the brahmin Aggibhāradvāja: "Do you know, brahmin, what an outcast is or the qualities that make one an outcast?"

"I do not know, Master Gotama, what an outcast is or the qualities that make one an outcast. Please let Master Gotama teach me the Dhamma in such a way that I might come to know what an outcast is and the qualities that make one an outcast."

"In that case, brahmin, listen and attend closely. I will speak."

"Yes, sir," the brahmin Aggibhāradvāja replied. The Blessed One said this:

> "A man who is angry and hostile,
> an evil denigrator,
> deficient in view, a hypocrite:
> you should know him as an outcast.
>
> "One here who injures a living being
> whether once-born or twice-born,
> who has no kindness toward living beings:
> you should know him as an outcast. . . .
>
> "One who extols himself
> and despises others,
> inferior because of his own conceit:
> you should know him as an outcast.
>
> "A scold, stingy,
> of evil desires, miserly, a deceiver,
> one without moral shame or moral dread:
> you should know him as an outcast.
>
> "One who reviles the Buddha
> or his disciple,
> a wanderer or a householder:
> you should know him as an outcast. . . .
>
> "One is not an outcast by birth,
> nor by birth is one a brahmin.
> By action one becomes an outcast,
> by action one becomes a brahmin."

(from Sn I,7)

6. The State

(1) When Kings Are Unrighteous

"When kings are unrighteous, the royal vassals become unrighteous. When the royal vassals are unrighteous, brahmins and householders become unrighteous. When brahmins and householders are unrighteous, the people of the towns and countryside become unrighteous. When the people of the towns and countryside are unrighteous, the sun and moon proceed off course. When the sun and moon proceed off course, the constellations and the stars proceed off course. When the constellations and the stars proceed off course, day and night proceed off course . . . the months and fortnights proceed off course . . . the seasons and years proceed off course. When the seasons and years proceed off course, the winds blow off course and at random. When the winds blow off course and at random, the deities become upset. When the deities are upset, sufficient rain does not fall. When sufficient rain does not fall, the crops ripen irregularly. When people eat crops that ripen irregularly, they become short-lived, ugly, weak, and sickly.

"But when kings are righteous, the royal vassals become righteous. When the royal vassals are righteous, brahmins and householders become righteous. When brahmins and householders are righteous, the people of the towns and countryside become righteous. When the people of the towns and countryside are righteous, the sun and moon proceed on course. When the sun and moon proceed on course, the constellations and the stars proceed on course. When the constellations and the stars proceed on course, day and night proceed on course . . . the months and fortnights proceed on course . . . the seasons and years proceed on course. When the seasons and years proceed on course, the winds blow on course and dependably. When the winds blow on course and dependably, the deities do not become upset. When the deities are not upset, sufficient rain falls. When sufficient rain falls, the crops ripen in season. When people eat crops that ripen in season, they become long-lived, beautiful, strong, and healthy."

> When cattle are crossing a ford,
> if the chief bull goes crookedly,
> all the others go crookedly
> because their leader has gone crookedly.
> So too, among human beings,
> when the one considered the chief
> behaves unrighteously,
> other people do so as well.

The entire kingdom is dejected
if the king is unrighteous.

When cattle are crossing a ford
if the chief bull goes straight across,
all the others go straight across
because their leader has gone straight.
So too, among human beings,
when the one considered the chief
conducts himself righteously,
other people do so as well.
The entire kingdom rejoices
if the king is righteous.

(AN 4:70, NDB 458–59)

(2) War Breeds Enmity

King Ajātasattu of Magadha mobilized a four-division army and marched in the direction of Kāsi against King Pasenadi of Kosala. King Pasenadi heard this report, mobilized a four-division army, and launched a counter-march in the direction of Kāsi against King Ajātasattu. Then King Ajātasattu and King Pasenadi fought a battle, in which King Ajātasattu defeated King Pasenadi. King Pasenadi, defeated, retreated to his own capital of Sāvatthī.

Then, in the morning, a number of monks dressed and, taking their bowls and robes, entered Sāvatthī for alms. When they had walked for alms in Sāvatthī and had returned from their alms round, after the meal they approached the Blessed One and reported what had happened. [The Blessed One said:]

"Monks, King Ajātasattu of Magadha has evil friends. King Pasenadi of Kosala has good friends. Yet for this day, King Pasenadi, having been defeated, will sleep badly tonight.

"Victory breeds enmity,
The defeated one sleeps badly.
The peaceful one sleeps at ease,
Having abandoned victory and defeat."

[On a later occasion, when Pasenadi defeated Ajātasattu, the Blessed One said:]

"The fool thinks fortune is on his side
so long as his evil does not ripen,

but when the evil ripens
the fool incurs suffering.

"The killer begets a killer,
one who conquers, a conqueror.
The abuser begets abuse,
the reviler, one who reviles.
Thus by the unfolding of kamma
the plunderer is plundered."

(SN 3:14–15, CDB 177–78)

(3) The Wheel-Turning Monarch

The Blessed One said: "Monks, even a wheel-turning monarch, a just and righteous king, does not govern his realm without a co-regent."

A certain monk asked: "But who, Bhante, is the co-regent of the wheel-turning monarch, the just and righteous king?"

"It is the Dhamma, the law of righteousness," replied the Blessed One. "The wheel-turning monarch, the just and righteous king, relying on the Dhamma, honoring the Dhamma, esteeming and respecting it, with the Dhamma as his standard, banner, and sovereign, provides lawful protection, shelter, and safety for his own dependents. He provides lawful protection, shelter, and safety for the khattiyas attending on him; for his army, for the brahmins and householders, for the inhabitants of town and countryside, for ascetics and brahmins, for the beasts and birds. A wheel-turning monarch, a just and righteous king, who thus provides lawful protection, shelter, and safety for all, is the one who rules by Dhamma only. And that rule cannot be overthrown by any hostile human being."

(from AN 3:14, NDB 208–9)

(4) How a Wheel-Turning Monarch Conquers

"Here, when a head-anointed noble king has bathed his head on the *uposatha* day of the fifteenth[2] and has ascended to the upper palace chamber for the *uposatha*, there appears to him the divine wheel-treasure with its thousand spokes, its tire, and its nave, complete in every aspect. On seeing it, the head-anointed noble king thinks thus: 'Now it has been heard by me that when a head-anointed noble king has bathed his head on the *uposatha* day of the fifteenth and has ascended to the upper palace chamber for the *uposatha*, and there appears to him the divine wheel-treasure with its thousand spokes, its tire, and its nave, complete in every aspect, then that king becomes a wheel-turning monarch. Am I then a wheel-turning monarch?'

"Then the head-anointed noble king rises from his seat, and taking a water vessel in his left hand, he sprinkles the wheel-treasure with his right hand, saying: 'Turn forward, good wheel-treasure; triumph, good wheel-treasure!' Then the wheel-treasure turns forward rolling in the eastern direction and the wheel-turning monarch follows it with his four-constituent army. Now in whatever region the wheel-treasure pauses, there the wheel-turning monarch takes up his abode with his four-constituent army. And opposing kings in the east come to the wheel-turning monarch and speak thus: 'Come, great king; welcome, great king; command, great king; advise, great king.' The wheel-turning monarch speaks thus: 'You should not destroy life; you should not take what has not been given; you should not engage in sexual misconduct; you should not speak falsehood; you should not drink intoxicants; you should enjoy your accustomed enjoyments.' And the opposing kings in the east submit to the wheel-turning monarch.

"Then the wheel-treasure plunges into the eastern ocean and emerges again. And then it turns forward rolling in the southern direction. . . . And the opposing kings in the south submit to the wheel-turning monarch. Then the wheel-treasure plunges into the southern ocean and emerges again. And then it turns forward rolling in the western direction. . . . And the opposing kings in the west submit to the wheel-turning monarch. Then the wheel-treasure plunges into the western ocean and emerges again. And then it turns forward rolling in the northern direction. . . . And the opposing kings in the north submit to the wheel-turning monarch.

"Now when the wheel-treasure has triumphed over the earth to the ocean's edge, it returns to the royal capital and remains as if fixed on its axle at the gate of the wheel-turning monarch's inner palace, as an adornment to the gate of his inner palace. Such is the wheel-treasure that appears to a wheel-turning monarch."

(from MN 129, MLDB 1023–24; see too DN 26, LDB 397–98)

(5) The Monarch's Duties

[The Buddha is relating a story of the distant past:] "King Daḷhanemi sent for his eldest son, the crown prince, and said: 'My son, the sacred wheel-treasure has slipped from its position. And I have heard that when this happens to a wheel-turning monarch, he has not much longer to live. I have had my fill of human pleasures, now is the time to seek heavenly pleasures. You, my son, take over control of this land. I will shave off my hair and beard, put on ocher robes, and go forth from the household life into homelessness.' And, having installed his eldest son in due form as king, King Daḷhanemi shaved off his hair and beard, put on ocher robes, and went forth from the household life into homelessness. And, seven days after the royal sage had gone forth, the sacred wheel-treasure vanished.

"Then a certain man came to the new king and said: 'Sire, you should know that the sacred wheel-treasure has disappeared.' At this the king was grieved and felt sad. He went to his father, the royal sage, and told him the news. And the royal sage said to him: 'My son, you should not grieve or feel sad at the disappearance of the wheel-treasure. The wheel-treasure is not an heirloom from your fathers. But now, my son, you must turn yourself into a noble wheel-turner. And then it may come about that, if you perform the duties of a noble wheel-turning monarch, on the *uposatha* day of the fifteenth, when you have washed your head and gone up to the verandah on top of your palace for the *uposatha* day, the sacred wheel-treasure will appear to you, thousand-spoked, complete with rim, hub, and all accessories.'

"'But what, Sire, is the duty of a noble wheel-turning monarch?'

"'It is this, my son: Relying on the Dhamma, honoring the Dhamma, esteeming and respecting it, with the Dhamma as your standard, banner, and sovereign, you should provide lawful protection, shelter, and safety for your own dependents. You should provide lawful protection, shelter, and safety for the khattiyas attending on you; for your army, for the brahmins and householders, for the inhabitants of town and countryside, for ascetics and brahmins, for the beasts and birds. Let no crime prevail in your kingdom, and to those who are in need, give wealth. And whatever ascetics and brahmins in your kingdom have renounced the life of sensual infatuation and are devoted to forbearance and gentleness, each one taming himself, each one calming himself, and each one striving for the end of craving, from time to time you should approach them and ask: "What, Bhante, is wholesome and what is unwholesome, what is blameworthy and what is blameless, what is to be followed and what is not to be followed? What deed will in the long run lead to harm and sorrow, and what to welfare and happiness?" Having listened to them, you should avoid what is unwholesome and do what is wholesome. That, my son, is the duty of a noble wheel-turning monarch.'

"'Yes, sire,' he said, and he performed the duties of a noble wheel-turning monarch. And so in succession six subsequent kings arose who became wheel-turning monarchs. Then the seventh king to arise in this dynasty did not go to the royal sage [his father, the former monarch] and ask him about the duties of a wheel-turning monarch. Instead, he ruled the people according to his own ideas, and being so ruled, the people did not prosper so well as they had done under the previous kings who had performed the duties of a wheel-turning monarch.

"The king then ordered all his ministers and advisers to come together, and he consulted them. And they explained to him the duties of a wheel-turning monarch. And having listened to them, the king established guard and protection for his subjects, but he did not give wealth to the needy, and as a result, poverty became rife. Thus, from the not giving of wealth to the needy, poverty became rife. From the growth of poverty, theft increased. From the increase of theft, the use of weapons increased; from the increased use of weapons, the taking of life increased, lying increased, divisive speech increased, and sexual misconduct increased—and on account of this, people's life- span decreased and their beauty decreased."

(from DN 26, LDB 396–401, abridged)

(6) Providing for the Welfare of the People

The Blessed One told the brahmin Kūṭadanta: "Brahmin, once upon a time there was a king called Mahāvijita. He was rich, of great wealth and resources, with an abundance of gold and silver, of possessions and requisites, of money and money's worth, with a full treasury and granary. And when King Mahāvijita was reflecting in private, the thought came to him: 'I have acquired extensive wealth in human terms, I occupy a wide extent of land which I have conquered. Let me now make a great sacrifice that would be to my benefit and happiness for a long time.' And calling his chaplain, he told him his thought. 'I want to make a great sacrifice. Instruct me, Bhante, how this may be to my lasting benefit and happiness.'

"The chaplain replied: 'Your Majesty's country is beset by thieves. It is ravaged; villages and towns are being destroyed; the countryside is infested with brigands. If Your Majesty were to tax this region, that would be the wrong thing to do. Suppose Your Majesty were to think: "I will get rid of this plague of robbers by executions and imprisonment, or by fines, threats, and banishment," the plague would not be properly ended. Those who survived would later harm Your Majesty's realm. However, with this plan you can completely eliminate the plague. To those in the kingdom who are engaged in cultivating crops and raising cattle, distribute grain and fodder; to those in trade, give capital; to those in government service, assign proper living wages. Then those people, being intent on their own occupations, will not harm the kingdom. Your Majesty's revenues will be great; the land will be tranquil and not beset by thieves; and the people, with joy in their hearts, playing with their children, will dwell in open houses.'

"And saying: 'So be it!,' the king accepted the chaplain's advice: he gave grain and fodder to those engaged in cultivating crops and raising cattle, capital to those in trade, proper living wages to those in government service. Then those people, being intent on their own occupations, did not harm the kingdom. The king's revenues became great; the land was tranquil and not beset by thieves; and the people, with joy in their hearts, playing with their children, dwelt in open houses."

(from DN 5, LDB 135–36)

Epilogue

BY HOZAN ALAN SENAUKE

If Shakyamuni Buddha is the Great Physician, then his teachings are medicine we need to bring our lives into balance and harmony. Medicine is of no use if it remains in the cabinet. Teachings and texts are of no benefit if they sit unopened on a shelf. Medicine and teachings alike must be taken into our bodies and mind, where they can catalyze freedom from suffering.

When Bhikkhu Bodhi shared with me the manuscript of this book (under its original title, *Fostering Social Harmony*), it was clear that this collection would have wide appeal to Buddhists in Asia and in the West, those who understand that *dukkha* is personally *and* socially constructed. No individual lives apart from the mutual influence of community, society, and nation. Society exists as the co-construction of all who live within it. Though technology ever accelerates the pace and scope of human connection and division, the social reality of mutual co-creation was as true in the Buddha's time and place as it is in ours.

I was right about the book's appeal. When I showed friends a printout of *Fostering Social Harmony* they were invariably eager to get a copy. With Bhikkhu Bodhi's permission, very limited Burmese and English editions of the earlier version were published inside Myanmar in 2014. Queries about publication in local languages have since come from Thailand, Sri Lanka, India, and Japan. All this is encouraging, but the question remains: How might we use these teachings as good medicine to foster social harmony?

Over the last few years of teaching I have explored this question. My own Buddhist roots grow from the Mahayana soil of Zen Buddhism. From high school I have been a social activist, and that has continued now into my late sixties in ways that feel resonant with the Dharma. For nearly twenty-five years I have been closely involved with the Buddhist Peace Fellowship and the International Network of Engaged Buddhists, two respected organizational voices for socially engaged Buddhism. By personal inclination I have always been an internationalist, seeing the inverted linkages between the wealth and privilege of the West and the poverty of many millions around the world. Through the circles of BPF and INEB I have come into close contact with the suffering of those less privileged than I, and with their great faith in the liberative potential of the Buddhadhamma.

This is particularly true in India, where a Buddhist revival has given rise to a powerful movement in the land of the Buddha's birth. This movement, inspired in the mid-twentieth century by a visionary social and religious leader, B. R. Ambedkar, has its roots in communities of India's most oppressed, those who for thousands of years had been classified from birth as untouchable. I work among these Ambedkarite Buddhists, and with them I have explored how to use the contents of this book as living teachings. In this epilogue I will share a picture of these communities and how we studied the Buddha's social teachings.

Because this emerging Indian Buddhism is little known in the West, to begin with I offer some background. Twenty-five hundred years ago, when the Buddha was enlightened, a community that included monks and nuns, laymen and laywomen, of all castes formed around him. A hereditary caste system, based on occupation and skin color, was already in place by the Buddha's time. It has since evolved into a complex and hierarchical social system of graded inequality. At the top of the pyramid are the *brahmins* or priests. The Buddha himself was born into the warrior caste, the *kshatriyas*. Below them is a merchant and agriculturalist caste, the *vaishyas*. *Shudras* are laborers and servants. And below them were Untouchables, more recently called *Dalits*, meaning, in Hindi and Marathi, people "broken" or ground up in the wheels of oppression.[1] The Buddha's egalitarian vision included them all, but position and nobility were evaluated on the basis of ethical action and understanding. In the Suttanipāta (v. 142) the Buddha says:

> One is not an outcast by birth,
> nor by birth is one a brahmin.
> By action one becomes an outcast,
> by action one becomes a brahmin.

But Buddhism was subject to a reassertion of brahmanist values from the first millennium CE. Later it was systematically repressed by Muslim invaders from the twelfth century on, and so it more or less disappeared as a distinct cultural force in India. Of course there are remnants woven into the culture. The nineteenth-century discovery of storied Buddhist sites inspired the Sri Lankan Buddhist revivalist Anagarika Dharmapala to call for the renascence of Buddhism in India, toward which end he founded the Maha Bodhi Society.

However caste is still a defining element of Indian society. In *The Age of Kali* William Dalrymple writes:

In much of rural India, caste still defines not only what you wear, but where you live, what trade you follow, whom you marry, even the colour you paint your home. Every detail of life in the traditional Indian village, where 80 percent of Indians still live, is regulated.[2]

By the 1920s a new figure came to prominence, agitating for the human, religious, and economic rights of the Untouchables or Dalits, India's vast population of oppressed communities. B. R. Ambedkar was a powerful thinker and writer, who came from the untouchable Mahar caste in central India. By virtue of his brilliance, Ambedkar won scholarships to Elphinstone College in Bombay and went on to earn advanced degrees at Columbia University in New York and the London School of Economics. He returned from the West in the 1920s as one of the most educated men in colonial India, still facing the discrimination that has been the lot of all Untouchables.

In his university teaching and legal work Ambedkar became a passionate advocate for the Untouchables. Where Gandhi pursued an anticolonial and nationalist course, we can see Dr. Ambedkar as the leader of a civil rights movement. He worked to deconstruct caste oppression in India while the colonial regime persisted, until after World War II and the collapse of Britain's empire, and into the first decade of India's independence. Despite sharp conflicts with Gandhi, following independence Ambedkar was chosen as India's first Law Minister. He is generally seen as the "father of the Indian constitution," a visionary document even today.

By the 1930s Ambedkar concluded that the dominant Hindu religion, with its inherent caste discrimination, was not likely to respond to political or religious reform. At the 1935 Yeola Conference of Depressed Classes, Ambedkar declared: "I was born a Hindu, but I solemnly assure you that I will not die as a Hindu." Over the next decade he investigated Islam, Christianity, and Sikhism—and was courted by each of these groups, who were well aware that Ambedkar's conversion would bring along with him millions of Untouchables and the promise of wide political power. But it was Buddhism, indigenous to India, open to all, and profoundly rational, that won his heart and mind.

By 1956, feeling the shadow of mortality, B. R. Ambedkar organized his conversion to Buddhism. On October 14, 1956, at the Deekshabhoomi (Conversion Ground) in Nagpur, he took the Three Refuges in the Buddha, the Dharma, and the Sangha, and received the five ethical precepts from the senior Thera-vadin Buddhist monk in India, U Chandramani. Then Ambedkar did an unprecedented thing, particularly unprecedented for a Buddhist layperson. Turning to four hundred thousand Untouchable followers who were present, he offered them the refuges and his own twenty-two vows, which included the five precepts and the renunciation of specific articles of Hindu practice and belief. This act of conscious conversion signaled a momentous renewal of Buddhism in India. A number of mass conversions followed within weeks, transforming the spiritual identity of millions of Dalits. But by early December, less than two months later, Dr. Ambedkar had died, succumbing to complications of diabetes and heart disease.

Nearly sixty years later Buddhism is still taking root among Dalit communities. Roadside viharas and modest temples can be found in all corners of the country. A 2012 Pew Research report puts the population of Indian Buddhists near ten million. Undeclared Buddhists greatly increase that number. But caste discrimination—with daily atrocities and murders against the poorest of the poor—remains a bitter and violent fact of Indian life. The goal of social harmony, so clearly articulated by the Buddha and by Dr. Ambedkar, is as yet a distant dream.

Nagaloka, in Nagpur where the first conversion ceremony took place, is a fifteen-acre campus dedicated to the unity of Buddhism and social change, in keeping with Ambedkar's vision. The physical heart of this peaceful campus is a forty-foot golden Buddha, sculpted as striding determinedly with his hand raised in the *abhaya mudra*, generating safety, dispelling fear. Within Nagaloka there is a residential training program, the Nagarjuna Training Institute, teaching young people meditation, basic Buddhism, social organizing, and the work of Dr. Ambedkar. Since 2002 more than eight hundred young women and men between seventeen and twenty-five, coming from almost every Indian state, have completed NTI's nine-month program. Many continue in residence and study a second or third year before returning to their home region or going on to higher education.

I have been working with these young people over the last six years. My ongoing effort is to provide economic support for NTI students, raising funds in the West by sharing my experience of the social and spiritual vitality of this "new" Indian Buddhism. Each time I visit Nagaloka I offer a short but intensive course that explores the territory where Buddhist practice and social action meet. We have done units on gender in the history of Buddhism and in contemporary Indian society; race, caste, and discrimination—looking at the U.S. Civil Rights movement and Indian untouchability; storytelling as a method for crossing social barriers; and Dr. Ambedkar's Buddhist teachings.

In November 2014 I used this book as our core text, drawing from several key sections in the course of a week:

- Right Understanding
- Community

- Proper Speech
- Anger
- Disputes and Settling Disputes

The teachings in these sections, and throughout *The Buddha's Teachings on Social and Communal Harmony*, are quite clear in language and intent. Step by step they point practitioners away from what is unwholesome and toward the wholesome. But in the classroom we met a challenge. As Bhikkhu Bodhi has suggested in conversation, we found that the Sutta Piṭaka is short on ambiguity—and the world we live in is not. To put this another way, our classroom discussions, beginning with the unambiguous canonical text, quickly arrived at circumstances in which wholesome choices were not so easy to identify. Without the diamond-cutting wisdom of a Buddha, we often found ourselves in uncertainty, aware of our mixed motivations.

Actually, a ground of ambiguity is set out in the third paragraph of the very first chapter, "Right View," drawn from the Majjhima Nikāya:

> Right view, I say, is twofold: there is right view that is affected by influxes, partaking of merit, ripening in the acquisitions; and there is right view that is noble, free of influxes, supramundane, a factor of the path.

"Right view affected by influxes" implies that even as we attempt to see and act in accord with the Dharma, we are still affected by the delusion of self. "Partaking of merit" is using Buddhist practice for what we perceive as our own benefit. "Ripening in the acquisitions" means becoming or acquiring a self. These are mundane or worldly ways. Right view as a factor of the noble eightfold path is noble, free of influxes or unstained, and supramundane, beyond the traps and snares of this world.

Note that the Buddha does not say that worldly or mundane right view is equivalent to wrong view, which would be an absolutist stance. His case might be more that right view affected by influxes is a good start . . . keep going. Right view that is free of influxes and supramundane is the view of wisdom and the clarity of keeping the Dharma in mind. Take that as a goal.

The following section, also from the Majjhima Nikāya, explains how to practice with what is unwholesome, meaning our actions rooted in greed, hate, and delusion, actions that set one person against another. He asks, "What is the root of the unwholesome?"

> The destruction of life is unwholesome; taking what is not given is unwholesome; sexual misconduct is unwholesome; false speech is unwholesome; divisive speech is unwholesome; harsh

speech is unwholesome; idle chatter is unwholesome; covetousness is unwholesome; ill will is unwholesome; wrong view is unwholesome.

We recognize these as a version of the basic Buddhist precepts, the moral foundation of our practice. The practice of what is wholesome is simply refraining from these habitual acts, which is easier said than done.

Of course we begin in this world, with all our incomplete views and difficult relationships. At first the NTI students found this discouraging. We humans often want a set of divine instructions, signposts showing us the right way. Instead, our classroom discussion placed us in the complexity of real life and threw each of us back on our own judgment, experience, and wisdom.

This was clear when we took up the Buddha's teaching on speech. These and similar instructions appear at several points in the body of Pāli suttas.

> Monks, possessing five factors, speech is well spoken, not badly spoken; it is blameless and beyond reproach by the wise. What five? It is spoken at the proper time; what is said is true; it is spoken gently; what is said is beneficial; it is spoken with a mind of loving-kindness. Possessing these five factors, speech is well spoken, not badly spoken; it is blameless and beyond reproach by the wise. (AN 5:198)

So the Buddha's conditions for proper speech call for words that are timely, true, gentle, beneficial or useful, and motivated by loving-kindness. The Nagaloka students, who practice a traditional loving-kindness meditation daily, were quick to agree to these instructions, but I raised a series of questions.

How does one know what is "timely"? If I am involved in a conflict with a friend, what is timely for me may not be so for my friend. What is "true"? We know that the truth is (almost) always a subjective matter. My own experience as a mediator is that two people often have mutually contradictory versions of the "truth."

"Gentle" and "beneficial" are similarly subjective. As Bhikkhu Bodhi points out in his introduction to Part IV (p. 73):

> . . . while the discourses stress the importance of establishing a gentle and compassionate attitude before criticizing others, they do not advocate speaking to others only in agreeable ways. To the contrary, they advise one to censure others when criticism is due.

A Buddha, with powers of omniscience, would not be guessing. But for most of us here in *saṃsāra* these four conditions of speech can be elusive. If

I know my friend well, I might be able to make a good guess about what she might perceive as timely, true, gentle, and useful. And I might guess wrongly. If my difference is with someone I don't know or with whom I already have a history of conflict, it is likely we will not agree on one or all of these points.

The fifth condition for proper speech is being "motivated by loving-kindness." While one can, of course, fool oneself about motivation, this is the aspect of speech that we can best know for ourselves. Using the Dhamma for investigation I can determine if my wish is to connect with another person or to separate myself from him or her. Am I turning toward sentient beings or away from them?

This provoked a rich classroom discussion about speech—what we say to one another, when, and why. The value of this discussion was not that all the students came to consensus on the issue, but that we were able to have an energetic conversation and enjoy it. The students noticed that they could hold different views—agree and disagree—while remaining in relationship with each other. This is the first step toward a society that is based on critical thinking.

As we read other sections of *Fostering Social Harmony* similar issues arose. Investigating the ten "grounds for resentment"—see **III,4** of the present volume—led to a lively debate about whether anger is understandable in the face of violence and oppressive social systems, and whether such anger is ever useful.

The chapter on "the intentional community" contains an excerpt from the Aṅguttara Nikāya's "Book of the Sevens"—here **VII,3(5)**—in which the Buddha preaches the seven conditions for social harmony to the ancient North Indian Licchavis or Vajjis. Included is an admonition that "as long as the Vajjis do not abduct women and girls from their families and force them to live with them, only growth is to be expected for them, not decline." This point touched off a passionate discussion about rape, the trafficking of women, gender oppression, and fear in the Nagaloka students' own communities.

I saw these Indian students using the Buddha's teaching not as dogma or doctrine, but as a guide for looking at the complexities of their real-life situations. They were learning to think for themselves and to accept a diversity of views by using the Dhamma itself.

In a 1950 essay, "Buddha and the Future of His Religion," Dr. Ambedkar considered the conversion of Dalit communities from untouchability to Buddhism. He saw a spiritual tradition grounded in critical thinking:

> [The Buddha] told Ananda that his religion was based on reason and experience and that his followers should not accept his teaching as correct and binding merely because they emanated from him. Being based on reason and experience they were free to

modify or even to abandon any of his teachings if it was found that at a given time and in given circumstances they do not apply. . . . He wanted that it should remain evergreen and serviceable at all times. . . . No other religious teacher has shown such courage.

The plight of India's Buddhists is particular to their cultural circumstances. But the many-sided discourse I describe, using *The Buddha's Teachings on Social and Communal Harmony* as a jumping-off point, is inevitable. I've had the same kind of provocative discussions in Burma and in the U.S. Reality can't be encompassed by truisms. Even well-intentioned people can hold a diversity of views. Yet a true vision of social harmony and tolerance points to a more peaceful world.

In a practical sense, developing our intention to connect is the key, which is done through training and practice of these teachings. Again and again the Buddha speaks to the challenge and necessity of this practice. He says:

> One who repays an angry man with anger
> thereby makes things worse for himself.
> Not repaying an angry man with anger,
> one wins a battle hard to win.
>
> He practices for the welfare of both—
> his own and the other's—
> when, knowing that his foe is angry,
> he mindfully maintains his peace.
>
> When he achieves the cure of both—
> his own and the other's—
> the people who consider him a fool
> are unskilled in the Dhamma.

Through our diligent effort, may we learn to find harmony even in times of conflict. As we grow in wisdom may we reflect that our "land was tranquil and not beset by thieves, and the people, with joy in their hearts, playing with their children, dwelt in open houses."

Notes

I: Right Understanding

1. These three types of wrong views and their counterparts are explored and analyzed in MN 60. They are also found at DN 2, MN 76, and elsewhere in the Nikāyas. In DN 2, moral nihilism is ascribed to a thinker named Ajita Kesakambalī; the doctrine of non-doing to Pūraṇa Kassapa; and the doctrine of non-causality to Makkhali Gosāla.
2. The three influxes (*āsava*) are sensual desire, desire for continued existence, and ignorance. The acquisitions (*upadhi*) are the five aggregates of clinging that constitute individual identity. Right view affected by influxes is a constituent of the mundane path conducive to a fortunate rebirth within *saṃsāra*, the continuum of birth and death. Right view free of influxes is the world-transcending wisdom that disrupts the continuum of birth and death.

II: Personal Training

1. See AN 10:103, NDB 1485.
2. In Pāli: *mettā, karuṇā, muditā*, and *upekkhā*.
3. For details, see Vism 318, Ppn 9.93–96.
4. Similar reflections are to be applied to verbal action and mental action, except that unwholesome mental actions are not to be confessed but to be regretted and avoided in the future.
5. *Sallekha.* The elimination of defilements.
6. The Buddha is here speaking to a young brahmin who asked about the path to union with Brahmā, the creator god of the brahmin belief system.
7. "No limiting kamma remains there" (*yaṃ pamāṇakataṃ kammaṃ na taṃ tatrāvasissati*): According to the commentary, this means that kamma pertaining to the sense sphere cannot prevent the kamma created by this "liberation of mind" from yielding its result, from producing rebirth in the brahma world, the divine world of the form realm: "Just as a flood overwhelms a puddle of water, so the wholesome kamma of this meditative absorption on loving-kindness surpasses in its power all the kamma of the sense sphere."
8. According to the commentary, what prevents this practitioner from attaining arahantship is attachment to the "*dhamma*" of concentration and insight. The five lower fetters (*pañc'orambhāgiyāni saṃyojanāni*) are: the view of a substantial self, doubt, seizing upon rules and observances, sensual lust, and ill will. With the eradication of these fetters, one becomes a non-returner (*anāgāmī*),

who takes spontaneous rebirth in the form realm (*rūpadhātu*) and attains final liberation there, without ever returning to the sensory realm.

III: Dealing with Anger

1. Dhp 184: *Khantī paramaṃ tapo titikkhā.*
2. The knowledge of one's own past lives, the knowledge of how others pass away and take rebirth according to their kamma, and the knowledge of the destruction of the influxes, that is, arahantship.

IV: Proper Speech

1. *Parato ghosa.* The other condition is careful reflection (*yoniso manasikāra*). See AN 2:126 (NDB 178).
2. The statement occurs at DN II 104–5 (LDB 246–47), SN V 261–62 (CDB 1724–25), AN IV 310–11 (NDB 1214–15), and Ud 63–64.
3. These are the four methods of formulating questions; see AN 4:42. The commentary explains: "(1) A *question that should be answered categorically* (*ekaṃsavyākaṇanīya pañha*) is, for example, 'Is the eye impermanent?' which should be answered categorically with 'Yes, it is impermanent.' (2) A *question that should be answered after making a distinction* (*vibhajjavyākaraṇīya pañha*) is, for example, 'Is the impermanent the eye?' which should be answered by making a distinction: 'Not only the eye, but the ear, nose, etc., are also impermanent.' (3) A question that should be answered with a counter-question (*paṭipucchāvyākaraṇīya pañha*) is, for example, 'Does the eye have the same nature as the ear?' One should answer this by asking, 'With respect to what?' If they reply, 'With respect to seeing,' one should answer no. If they reply, 'With respect to impermanence,' one should answer yes. (4) A question that should be set aside (*ṭhapanīya pañha*) is, for example, 'Is the soul the same as the body?' This should be set aside without answering it, saying, 'This has not been declared by the Tathāgata.'"
4. The meaning of these expressions is far from self-evident. My translation relies on the explanation given in the commentary. For details, see NDB note 465, pp. 1654ff.
5. That is, he seizes upon a slight mistake on the other's part as a pretext for criticizing him.
6. The commentary explains: "He directly knows one thing, the noble path. He fully understands one thing, the truth of suffering. He abandons one thing, all unwholesome qualities. He realizes one thing, the fruit of arahantship or cessation [nibbāna]. By means of knowledge he reaches right liberation, emancipation by the fruit of arahantship."

V: Good Friendship

1. Sn 261: *asevanā ca bālānaṃ paṇḍitānañ ca sevanā.*
2. See, for example, the refrain in SN 22:35–36 and SN 22:63–70.
3. For the six paired suttas extolling the role of good friendship in facilitating

the attainment of the path, see SN 45:49 and 45:56, SN 45:63 and 45:70, and SN 45:77 and 45:80 (CDB pp. 1543–48).

4. On the mutual duties of preceptor and pupils, see especially Vin I 46–53 (BD 4:59–69).

5. The code of monastic rules.

VII: The Intentional Community

1. In the section of AN from which these passages are extracted, ten pairs of communities are described. I have selected these five as most pertinent to the theme of this book.

2. See DN 16.6.1 (LDB 269–70).

3. For details, see Ṭhānissaro Bhikkhu, *The Buddhist Monastic Code II*, chapter 12.

4. This conversation obviously takes place after the Buddha's passing. The brahmin Vassakāra was the chief minister of King Ajātasattu of Magadha. Perhaps he inquired from Ānanda about the administration of the monastic order because he was aware of the intense violence that takes place over the right to the throne. Ajātasattu had his father executed in order to achieve kingship, and he in turn was killed by his own son.

5. The *uposatha*, the days of the full moon and the new moon, when monastics gather to recite the Pātimokkha, the monastic code, and laypeople often take extra precepts.

6. Better known by the Sanskrit terms *kshatriya, brāhmaṇa, vaishya,* and *śūdra*.

VIII: Disputes

1. The full account of the quarrel at Kosambī is told in the Vinaya Piṭaka in Mahāvagga, chapter X; see BD 4:483–513. See too in this connection MN 48.

2. *Papañcasaññāsaṅkhā.* This pithy term, not defined in the Nikāyas, seems to refer to perceptions and ideas that have become "infected" by subjective biases, "elaborated" by the tendencies to craving, conceit, and distorted views. According to the commentaries, craving, conceit, and views are the three factors responsible for conceptual elaboration (*papañca*).

3. The nine terms rooted in craving, with explanations from the commentary in parenthesis, are: (1) *pariyesanā* (seeking objects such as forms); (2) *lābha* (obtaining objects such as forms); (3) *vinicchaya* (deciding what is desirable and undesirable, beautiful and ordinary, how much to keep and how much to give away, how much to use and how much to save, etc.); (4) *chandarāga* (weak lust and strong lust, respectively); (5) *ajjhosāna* (the strong conviction in "I" and "mine"); (6) *pariggaha* (taking possession by way of craving and views); (7) *macchariya* (unwillingness to share with others); (8) *ārakkha* (guarding carefully); (9) *daṇḍādāna*, etc. (the taking up of weapons to ward off others).

IX: Settling Disputes

1. The procedures of overturning the almsbowl and turning it upright are authorized at Vin II 124–27. See Ṭhānissaro, *The Buddhist Monastic Code II*, pp. 411–12.

The commentary explains that the monks do not actually turn the almsbowl upside down before the lay follower but approve a motion not to accept gifts from him. Similarly, they abolish this act by approving a motion to receive his gifts again. The procedure of overturning the almsbowl was used in Myanmar in late 2007 when monks imposed such a penalty on the military junta. To express disapproval of the generals they walked down the streets with their bowls actually turned upside down.

2. For nuns, eight expulsion offenses have been laid down.

3. I take *abhidhamme* here to refer, not to the collection of treatises that constitute the Abhidhamma Piṭaka or its philosophy, but simply to the Dhamma itself, with the prefix *abhi–* serving a purely referential function, in the sense of "about, concerning, pertaining to."

4. Nātaputta, also known as Mahāvīra, was the head of the Jain community at the time and is often regarded as the historical founder of Jainism, though it is likely he was continuing a lineage of teachers that had started much earlier.

5. There are four kinds of disciplinary issues: involving a dispute (*vivādādhikaraṇa*); involving an accusation (*anuvādādhikaraṇa*); involving an offense (*āpattādhikaraṇa*); and involving procedure (*kiccādhikaraṇa*). These are dealt with in detail at Vin II 88–92. Briefly, an issue involving a dispute arises when monks or nuns dispute about the Dhamma and the Vinaya; an issue involving an accusation arises when one accuses another member of committing a transgression; an issue involving an offense arises when a monk or nun who has committed a transgression seeks rehabilitation; and an issue involving procedure deals with the collective procedures of the Sangha. The passage cited here deals with methods of settling disputes.

6. *Dhammanetti samanumajjitabbā*. The commentary provides various explanations of how to apply the guideline of the Dhamma, from the standpoint of both the suttas and the Vinaya.

7. The commentary explains the expression "not settled internally" (*ajjhattaṃ avūpasantaṃ*) thus: "Not settled in one's own mind and in one's own circle of pupils and students."

8. *Appasāda*. When this has been proclaimed, they need not rise up from their seat for him, or pay homage to him, or go out to meet him, or give him gifts.

9. *Paṭisāraṇiyakamma*. When this is imposed, the monk must go to the householder, accompanied by another monk, and apologize. If he fails to win the householder's forgiveness, his companion should try to reconcile them. The background story is at Vin II 15–18, with the legal stipulations at Vin II 18–21. For details, see Ṭhānissaro, *The Buddhist Monastic Code II*, pp. 407–11.

10. The commentary does not offer an explanation of this expression, but the implication seems to be that the troublesome monk, by his behavior, is not a real disciple of the Buddha and thus can be considered a "son" (that is, a disciple) of another teacher.

X: Establishing an Equitable Society

1. *Dānaṃ sīlaṃ pariccāgaṃ, ajjavaṃ maddavaṃ tapaṃ; akkodhaṃ avihiṃsañca, khantiñca avirodhanaṃ.*

2. The fifteenth of the lunar fortnight, the full-moon day, set apart for special religious observances.

Epilogue

1. For more detail on the Dalits, the former "Untouchables," Dr. Ambedkar, the "new" Buddhist movement in India, and the students with whom I have worked, see my book *Heirs To Ambedkar: The Rebirth of Engaged Buddhism in India* (Berkeley: Clear View Press, 2013).
2. William Dalrymple, *The Age of Kali: Indian Travels and Encounters* (New York: Penguin, 1998), 115.

Bibliography

PRIMARY SOURCES

Bodhi, Bhikkhu, trans. *The Connected Discourses of the Buddha: A Translation of the Saṃyutta Nikāya*. Boston: Wisdom Publications, 2000.

———, trans. *The Numerical Discourses of the Buddha: A Translation of the Aṅguttara Nikāya*. Boston: Wisdom Publications, 2012.

———, trans. *The Suttanipāta* (in preparation).

Buddharakkhita, Acharya, trans. *The Dhammapada: The Buddha's Path of Wisdom*. 2nd ed. Kandy, Sri Lanka: Buddhist Publication Society, 1996.

Horner, I. B., trans. *The Book of Discipline*, vols. 1–6. London: Pali Text Society (1969–75).

Ireland, John D., trans. *The Udāna and the Itivuttaka: Inspired Utterances of the Buddha and The Buddha's Sayings*. Kandy, Sri Lanka: Buddhist Publication Society, 1997.

Ñāṇamoli, Bhikkhu, trans. *The Path of Purification: Visuddhimagga*. Onalaska: BPS Pariyatti Editions, 1991.

———, trans. *The Middle Length Discourses of the Buddha: A Translation of the Majjhima Nikāya*, edited by Bhikkhu Bodhi. 3rd ed. Boston: Wisdom Publications, 2005.

Walshe, Maurice, trans. *The Long Discourses of the Buddha: A Translation of the Dīgha Nikāya*. Boston: Wisdom Publications, 1995.

SEE ALSO:

Bodhi, Bhikkhu, compiler. *In the Buddha's Words, An Anthology of Discourses from the Pāli Canon*. Boston: Wisdom Publications, 2005.

Ṭhānissaro, Bhikkhu, trans. *The Buddhist Monastic Code, I and II*. 2nd ed. Valley Center: Metta Forest Monastery, 2007.

Index

A

actions (deeds):
  results. *See* results of actions
  social status as determined by,
    182–85
  See also good conduct; kamma
Ajātasattu vs. Pasenadi, 187–88
almsbowl: overturning/upturning,
  157, 204–5n1(IX)
altruistic joy. *See* joy
Ānanda, 89, 115–16, 150–51, 160–61
anger, 51–68
  dangers in, 53–56
  re disciplinary issues, 154
  harsh/sharp speech, 23, 36, 38, 68,
    81–82
  irrational/without reason, 53
  killing of, 51
  not repaying, 62
  person types re, 51–53
  persons prone to, 55–56
  removing/overcoming, 56–59. See
    also patience
  See also enmity; hatred; ill will;
    resentment
arguments. *See* disputes
assemblies in communities, 119, 120,
  124

B

bad conduct, 36
bad persons, 95–96
bad thoughts, 39
benevolence, 38, 40
  See also good conduct
blaming others, 80

blind men and the elephant, 133–34
body: impurity/purity by, 36, 37
brahmins, 176–78, 178–81
the Buddha:
  community leadership, 119–20
  political vision, 186–92
  rejection of abuse, 63
  successor issue, 115–16, 150–51
  three clear knowledges, 19–20, 64,
    202n2(III)

C

caring for the sick, 120–21
caste (caste system):
  hierarchy, 176–78, 178–81
  as irrelevant in the monastic com-
    munity, 121–23
  See also outcasts
  communities. *See* intentional com-
    munities; lay community; monas-
    tic community
compassion, 42, 146
concord in the Sangha, 138
contentment (noncovetousness), 38,
  118
cordiality, principles of, 117–19
correction of transgressions, 149
  accepting from others, 155–57
  ease of, and social harmony, 118
  mutual correction, 154–55
  patience vs. punishment, 60–62
"covering over with grass," 152
covetousness (greed), 37, 38–39
craving. *See* desire
criticism: giving and receiving, 80,
  81–82

About the Editor

Bhikkhu Bodhi is an American Buddhist monk from New York City, born in 1944. He obtained a BA in philosophy from Brooklyn College and a PhD in philosophy from Claremont Graduate School. After completing his university studies he traveled to Sri Lanka, where he received novice ordination in 1972 and full ordination in 1973, both under the leading Sri Lankan scholar-monk, Balangoda Ananda Maitreya (1896–1998). From 1984 to 2002 he was the editor for the Buddhist Publication Society in Kandy, where he lived for ten years with the senior German monk Nyanaponika Thera (1901–94) at the Forest Hermitage. He returned to the U.S. in 2002. He currently lives and teaches at Chuang Yen Monastery in Carmel, New York. Bhikkhu Bodhi has many important publications to his credit, either as author, translator, or editor, including the definitive English-language editions of the Nikayas. In 2008, together with several of his students, Bhikkhu Bodhi founded Buddhist Global Relief, a non-profit supporting hunger relief, sustainable agriculture, and education in countries suffering from chronic poverty and malnutrition.

About Wisdom Publications

Wisdom Publications is the leading publisher of classic and contemporary Buddhist books and practical works on mindfulness. To learn more about us or to explore our other books, please visit our website at wisdompubs.org or contact us at the address below.

Wisdom Publications
199 Elm Street
Somerville, MA 02144 USA

We are a 501(c)(3) organization, and donations in support of our mission are tax deductible.

Wisdom Publications is affiliated with the Foundation for the Preservation of the Mahayana Tradition (FPMT).

Thank you for supporting Wisdom!

Please visit wisdompubs.org/books/pali-canon
to read suttas from the Pāli Canon online.